BORN IN 1958?
WHAT ELSE HAPPENED?

RON WILLIAMS

AUSTRALIAN SOCIAL HISTORY

BOOK 20 IN A SERIES OF 30
FROM 1939 to 1968

War Babies Years (1939 to 1945):   7 Titles
Baby Boom Years (1946 to 1960):   15 Titles
Post Boom Years (1961 to 1968):   8 Titles

BOOM, BOOM BABY, BOOM

Published by Boom Books. Wickham, NSW, Australia
Web: www.boombooks.biz   Email: email@boombooks.biz

Distributed by Woodslane Pty Ltd. Warriewood, NSW.
Phone: (02) 8445 2300. E: info@woodslane.com.au

© Ron Williams 2017

A single chapter or part thereof may be copied and reproduced without permission, provided that the Author, Title, and Web Site are acknowledged.

Creator: Williams, Ron, 1934- author
Title: Born in 1958? : what else happened? / Ron Williams.
Edition: Premier edition
Series: Born in series, book 20.
Almanacs, Australian.
Australia--History--Miscellanea--20th century.
Dewey Number: 994.04

Some Letters used in this text may still be in copyright. Every reasonable effort has been made to locate the writers. If any persons or their estates can establish authorship, and want to discuss copyright, please contact the author at email@boombooks.biz

Cover images: Syann Williams (personal copy); National Archives of Australia A1200, L26804, street scene; A12111, 1/1958/4/31, home building; A1200, L26428, Rugby League Australia v England; A12111, 1/1958/22/33, youngsters playing.

TABLE OF CONTENTS

JANUARY: IDLE THOUGHTS	3
CHURCHES AND GAMBLING	7
FEBRUARY: LASSETER'S GOLD	17
WHINGING POMS	19
MARCH: BREAD HANDLING	31
SCHOOL MILK	33
APRIL: ARTIFICAL UNSEMINATION	47
PUBS AND ART UNIONS	48
MAY: FUN ON SUNDAYS	59
COMPUTERS ARE COMING	64
JUNE: HURSEYS IN TASMANIA	71
THE DEATH PENALTY	76
JULY: THE MIDDLE EAST	87
MENACE OF HIRE PURCHASE	89
AUGUST: EMPIRE GAMES	99
AN ABORIGINE HELL-HOLE	102
SEPTEMBER: POLICE IN THE SPOTLIGHT	115
BIRTH CONTROL	122
OCTOBER: YOUTH IN THE SPOLIGHT	129
SP BETTING	133
NOVEMBER: FEDERAL ELECTIONS	139
ELECTRIC JUGS	144
DECEMBER: TIDYING UP THE HERSEYS	151
SUMMING UP 1958	158

IMPORTANT PEOPLE AND EVENTS

Queen of England	Elizabeth II
Prime Minister of Oz	Bob Menzies
Leader of Opposition	Doc Evatt
Governor General	Sir William Slim
The Pope, till October	Pius XII
The Pope, after October	John Paul XXIII
US President	Dwight Eisenhower
PM of Britain	Harold Macmillan

HOLDER OF THE ASHES

1956	England 2 - 1
1958 - 59	Australia 4 - 0
1961	Australia 2 - 1

MELBOURNE CUP WINNERS

1957	Straight Draw
1958	Baystone
1959	Macdougal

ACADEMY AWARDS

Best actor	David Niven
Best actress	Susan Hayward
Best Movie	Gigi

PREFACE TO THIS SERIES: 1939 to 1968

This book is the 20th in a series of books that I have researched and written. It tells a story about a number of important or newsworthy Australia-centric events that happened in 1958. The series covers each of the years from 1939 to 1968, for a total of thirty books.

I developed my interest in writing these books a few years ago at a time when my children entered their teens. My own teens started in 1947, and I started trying to remember what had happened to me then. I thought of the big events first, like Saturday afternoon at the pictures, and cricket in the back yard, and the wonderful fun of going to Maitland on the train for school each day. Then I recalled some of the not-so-good things. I was an altar boy, and that meant three or four Masses a week. I might have thought I loved God at that stage, but I really hated his Masses. And the schoolboy bullies, like Greg Barrell, and the hapless Freddie Evatt. Yet, to compensate for these, there was always the beautiful, black headed, blue-sailor-suited June Browne, who I was allowed to worship from a distance.

I also thought about my parents. Most of the major events that I lived through came to mind readily. But after that, I realised that I really knew very little about these parents of mine. They had been born about the start of the Twentieth Century, and they died in 1970 and 1980. For their last 20 years, I was old enough to speak with a bit of sense. I could have talked to them a lot about their lives. I could have found out about the times they lived in. But I did not. I know almost nothing about them really. Their courtship? Working in the pits? The Lock-out in the Depression?

Losing their second child? Being dusted as a miner? The shootings at Rothbury? My uncles killed in the War? There were hundreds, thousands of questions that I would now like to ask them. But, alas, I can't. It's too late.

Thus, prompted by my guilt, I resolved to write these books. They describe happenings that affected people, real people. In 1958, there is some coverage of international affairs, but a lot more on social events within Australia. This book, and the whole series is, to coin a modern phrase, designed to push the reader's buttons, to make you remember and wonder at things forgotten. The books might just let nostalgia see the light of day, so that oldies and youngies will talk about the past and re-discover a heritage otherwise forgotten. Hopefully, they will spark discussions between generations, and foster the asking and the answering of questions that should not remain unanswered.

The sources of my material. I was born in 1934, so that I can remember well a great deal of what went on around me from 1939 onwards. But of course, the bulk of this book's material came from research. That meant that I spent many hours in front of a computer reading electronic versions of newspapers, magazines, Hansard, Ministers' Press releases and the like. My task was to sift out, day-by-day, those stories and events that would be of interest to most readers. Then I supplemented these with materials from books, broadcasts, memoirs, biographies, government reports and statistics. And I talked to old-timers, one-on-one, and in organised groups, and to Baby Boomers about their recollections. People with stories to tell came out of the woodwork, and talked no end about the tragic, and funny, and commonplace events that have shaped their lives.

The presentation of each book. For each year covered, the end result is a collection of short Chapters on many of the topics that concerned ordinary people in that year. I think I have covered most of the major issues that people then were interested in. On the other hand, in some cases I have dwelt a little on minor frivolous matters, perhaps to the detriment of more sober considerations. Still, in the long run, this makes the book more readable, and hopefully it will convey adequately the spirit of the times.

Each of the books is mainly Sydney based, but I have been deliberately national in outlook, so that readers elsewhere will feel comfortable that I am talking about matters that affected them personally. After all, housing shortages and strikes and juvenile delinquency involved all Australians, and other issues, such as problems overseas, had no State component in them. Overall, I expect I can make you wonder, remember, rage and giggle equally, no matter where you hail from.

INTRO TO 1958

Bob Menzies had been Prime Minister since 1950, and indeed he would keep that position until he resigned, not out, in 1966. He was leader of the Liberal Party, and most of the time, he was secure in the job and had no fears of being ousted by the Opposition Labor Party.

This was because Labor was constantly, over the years, in a state of internal conflict. Every week, or every day, there was some story in the headlines of some Labor entity sacking members, or rebel groups forming and being routed, of some group or other being disciplined or expelled. Mixed in with this was problems with leadership.

The top man of the Party was Doc Evatt. He is often referred to as brilliant, but then comes the inevitable reference to the fact that he was erratic, and an impractical visionary. He had been the Chief Justice of the High Court, and had left there to enter politics. By 1957, he had badly blotted his copybook in the Petrov spy trial of 1956, and was always battling to maintain his leadership. His deputy, Arthur Calwell, was a pre-war thinker with strong attachment to the idea of a strong government, with all the powers of a socialist state. This was a concept that was not at all popular with voters, but Calwell never accepted that. It was often said that Labor would never regain office while these two men led it. This proved to be correct.

OUR BIG FRIEND OVERSEAS

Australia was a nation with a population of about 10 million. To the north of us, there were a dozen Asian nations with populations much larger, and China and India had over 500 million. So we were small fry. In fact, very small fry.

We needed friends in case one of our neighbours decided to conquer us and send its own people to live here. Up until the war, it was taken for granted that any aggressor would be fended off by Britain and the Empire. Since then it had become obvious that this type of protection no longer existed. Who, then, could we turn to?

The United States, of course, our WWII ally. So, over the years we had built our alliance with America. At times, this had galled many Australians, but wise heads knew that it was necessary for our long-term safety. So, one of the strategies that we stuck to was to follow the US in foreign policy no matter where it took us.

That meant that we fought alongside the Americans in the Korean war in 1951. It meant that we now refused to recognise the new nation of Red China, even though 90 per cent of the world, including Britain, had already accepted it. It meant that in another decade, we would send our men off to Vietnam to fight the Reds, in an unpopular war that served no purpose.

Wherever the US went, we followed. Menzies had no problems with this. Many people disagreed with it at times. But, they were not the Prime Minister.

THE REDS IN AUSTRALIA

Broadly speaking, at the time, there were two types of Communists in Australia. The first type, the die-hards, were greatly influenced by the revolution in Russia in 1917, and were intent on bringing to Australia a similar event, complete with the destruction of the economy, the seizure of all property, and the rolling on many heads in the gutter.

The second type were more moderate. They wanted the State to control many of the assets of the nation, and wanted it to have a large measure of control over people's lives. But they were not at all interested in a violent revolution. They were exaggerated socialists, just a step further along the path from many Labor men.

So that Labor was caught in a bad spot. They were all in favour of socialism, and the nationalisation of industry. But every time they opened their mouths to advocate for this, Menzies and his Party jumped on them and said that they were closet Communists wanting to turn Australia into Russia.

For all of the Menzies era, he used the Red scare tactics successfully and mercilessly. Whenever the good Prime Minister needed a boost in the polls, he pulled the "Reds under the beds" stunt and, sure enough, scared voters flocked to him for comfort.

The certainty of strikes. If any family round the nation was feeling insecure for any reason, it could draw solace from the fact that at least there was one thing that it could rely on. It knew that at some time over every week, it would be affected by one or more strikes. They might last for a day or two, or a month. They might stop the trains or buses, they might stop electricity, they might block the harbour, or shut down the pits or the mail. But, rest assured, there would be an array to choose from in any given week, and they would be freely available to everyone without favour.

All of this came by courtesy of the Reds. Their hard-liners had control of the Trade Unions, and were intent on destroying the economy of the nation. What better way was there than to call as many strikes as possible? Some of these, seeking better working conditions, were justified. The majority were certainly not, and were just expressions of the folly of the Union Reds.

All of this was annoying and frustrating to the man and woman in the street. And it doubtless had the same effect on Menzies, and he reacted at times with suitable policies to reduce the strike menace. At the same time, one small compensation for him was that he could use every strike, big or small, justified or not, to whip the Reds and their "fellow travellers", the Labor Party. So for him, and to use an old phrase, "every cloud had a silver lining."

Comment. The Reds in Australia at the time were just staring to lose a little of their industrial clout. They were still strong in the Unions, and led ferocious campaigns for better working conditions. But their attempts to gain power **through the electoral system** had never achieved anything at all, and by now it was generally agreed that they never would. So that individuals **as workers**, went along with their wage and conditions grabs, but **as voters** and citizens, they completely rejected the Reds and their policies of violent revolution.

THE ECONOMY OF THE NATION

The nation was doing well. Most people could easily get a job, wages were pretty good, housing was tight but gradually getting better. The banks were **often** lending, and Hire Purchase was very much on the increase. Most goods were available for sale, prices were moderate, and even the disadvantaged had a safety net that was adequate if not generous.

Of course, now and then the governments added taxes on beer and tobacco and perhaps luxury goods. They played round with sales tax, sometimes raising it, and sometimes cutting. Councils were expanding their services and always wanted more rates, and utilities **never** applied for a price reduction. In all though, for the average citizen, times were good, and Sunday barbies under the Hills Hoist were places of good cheer, with lots of steak and sausage sandwiches and a ton of beer.

There was one cloud loitering in our overseas situation. The Brits were talking all the time about joining some form of common market with the other nations of Europe. The consequences for us as a nation would be that if it did so, then our comfortable trade with Britain would be open to more competition, and so we would have to look round the world for other markets. This penny was dropping, slowly, but if the Brits really got serious, then we would be badly exposed. At the moment though, the Sunday barbies were not spoiled by such thoughts, and we could relax for a while in our comfortable and delightfully insular world.

EVENTS FROM 1957

One of the biggest events of 1957 was the Russian launching of the world's first satellite, known as Sputnik. This vehicle circled the earth, and went into orbit just like any planet. For many nights of the year, it became possible to watch it move across the sky, and know that several hours later it would be back for a repeat performance.

Apart from the new spectacle of people being able to watch the glowing contraption from their back yard, it shocked the Western world because it meant that the dreaded Reds were now at the forefront of **the space race**.

Prior to this, America and its Western allies had publicly poured scorn on Russian claims that it was a scientifically advanced nation. Any so-called advances emerging from Russia were pooh-poohed by the western Press as crude propaganda, and laughed away as nonsense. Here now, however, was undeniable evidence that the Russians were clearly in the lead in the most popular scientific game in town. Many people, here and especially in America, found this hard to take.

So western world official comments on the splendid feat were very restrained and cool. Most of them spoke not of the scientific break-throughs involved, but focused on the dangers that such satellites might present if used unwisely. Still, nothing daunted, the Russians responded in a few weeks by launching a second satellite. This one, though, had a dog on it. **Now a new craze swept the world.** The Russians said that they had created a rescue package that would eject the dog after about ten days, and parachute it to earth. Citizens round the world started counting the days, and waiting for this messiah-like dog to come to earth.

Unfortunately, the blessed event did not happen, and the dog presumably starved to death in space. Still, despite this disappointment, the double episode was a major propaganda victory for the Russians.

READY FOR 1958

We are just about ready for 1958. In the next few paragraphs, I give you my **Rules in Writing**. They include notes on how I handled the various inputs that I used, and what my position is on infallibility.

Apart from that, we are ready to go.

MY RULES IN WRITING THESE BOOKS

NOTE. Throughout this book, I rely a lot on reproducing **Letters from the newspapers**. Whenever I do this, I put the text in a different font, and indent it a little, and make the font somewhat smaller. I do not edit the text at all. That is, **I do not correct spelling or grammar,** and if the text gets at all garbled, I do not correct it. It's just as it was seen in the Papers.

SECOND NOTE. The material for this book, when it comes from newspapers, is reported as it was seen at the time. If the benefit of hindsight over the years changes things, then I might record that in my Comments. The info reported thus **reflects matters as they were seen at the time in 1958**.

THIRD NOTE. Let me also apologise in advance to anyone I might offend. In a work such as this, it is certain some people will think I got some things wrong. I am sure that I did, but please remember, all of this is only my opinion. And really, **my opinion does not matter one little bit in the scheme of things. I hope you will say "silly old bugger", shrug your shoulders, and read on.**

FOURTH NOTE. Let me remind you, though, that the writers of Letters to the newspapers did so mainly **with pen and ink**. In the early years, this was really laborious, with a pen and nib, and ink-bottle, and a blotter. Over the next thirty years, fountain pens became popular and then some early ball-points came on the scene. Whenever they wrote, it was quite a task, and the fact that they wrote so many Letters testifies to their passion.

JANUARY NEWS ITEMS

NSW had last year decided to **tear down some tram sheds and build an Opera House in their stead**. This was a grand vision and there were many doubts about how it could be financed. In the very long run, it was decided that **much of the money could come from the sale of special lotteries** that would cost more per ticket, and give bigger prizes than earlier lotteries....

Protestant churches in NSW launched a series of attacks on gambling. They were appalled at the huge interest in racetrack gambling on the new jackpot tote, and the number of sales of Lottery tickets....

They said that "gambling was reaching **terrifying** proportions", and that gambling was "the **greatest menace** to the social stability and moral welfare of the community". **Comment.** Despite an extensive campaign from the pulpit and elsewhere, the Opera House Lottery went from **success to success**.

January 4th. **A great Polar Race** is currently underway between New Zealand and Britain. The NZ team is led by **Sir Edmund Hillary**. Starting at the same time from "the South Ice base" they have been racing towards the South Pole since Christmas Day. **The distance will be about 500 miles....**

But this is **not the classical race of yesteryear**. They are **using powerful tractors** and covering about 50 miles per day. Scott's much earlier expedition using sleds covered about 8 miles per day....

It is expected that the race result of will be a neck-and-neck finish, though the Brits are slightly ahead at this date.

Australian Ray Lawler wrote a play two years ago called *The Summer of the 17th Doll*. It portrayed the visit of a Queensland cane cutter to Melbourne in his off-season. I saw it at the time and wrote to my parents saying that it was not worth travelling 30 miles to see it. Despite my expert advice, it was very successful in Australia, and **migrated to Britain well enough**....

The film rights to the play have been **sold in America for 360,000 US Dollars**. The movie will be made in Australia, and will star **Rita Hayworth and Burt Lancaster**....

Hayworth has just announced that she will marry producer James Hill. Her previous husbands were oil man Edward Judson, **Orson Welles, Prince Aly Khan, and crooner Dick Haymes**.

January 7th. Hillary's NZ team reached the Pole first. The Brits were tied up badly when the weather closed in.

Bluebottles at the beach are one of the delights to be expected now and then. But one lifesaver at Queensland's Tewantin Beach was not at all happy when **a monster bluebottle wrapped its eight-foot tentacles round him**, and clung on while he swam 50 yards to the shore. Once there, other lifesavers ripped the tentacles off. The young man was in severe pain for hours, but survived.

IDLE THOUGHTS IN THIS IDLE MONTH

One thing in the world is predictable. At the start of every year, dozens of politicians and churchmen and dignitaries will tell the ordinary citizens of this nation that the world has been a faulted place in the past, but if we are brave and earnest and ethical, then this coming year will be a rewarding one.

In the Western world, their messages are slanted towards trusting in the Christian god, not believing the fictions put out by the blasphemous Reds, and trusting in the government of the day.

These messages bring out many Letters, and some of the more conformist are published. Below is an example of the full-blown rhetoric that a New Year writer can get away with for a few days. Any other time of the year, the writer would be cut to ribbons.

Letters, H Wright. Her Majesty's Christmas broadcast presented a challenge which only a somnolent mind would disregard. It may not be a function of the Head of the Commonwealth to "give laws" or "administer justice," but such inability is surely more than off-set **when this beloved personality stands before millions of her subjects** to plead so sincerely for the exhibition of the type of courage which "makes us **stand up for everything that we know is right, everything that is true, and honest."**

May the clarion call be heard and heeded by many of the many people who "feel lost and unable to decide what to hold on to and what to discard" in a swiftly changing world.

The Queen's reference to the "ageless ideals" which unthinking people so carelessly throw away links her appeal with the inspired philosophy of the "king of kings" himself. The code of practical Christian ethics enunciated and exemplified by the Royal Child of Bethlehem supplies the framework for a way of life that cannot be excelled.

The man who espouses and practises these superlative principles of conduct will be making a maximum contribution towards ensuring for himself and for his fellow men "A Happy New Year"!

Our local Protestant churches take the opportunity to press their own missions. At the moment, they rail against betting on anything from horse racing, to two-up, on to lotteries, and right down to housie-housie. They hate the drinking of alcohol, and oppose reforms of the drinking laws that still allow **any** alcohol consumption. They deplore Sunday sport and the payments that go with it. Mostly they do not approve of teenage dancing, and if they do, then only on church premises under strict supervision.

Not everyone agreed that such matters warranted the attention of the churches. Mr Apthorpe below puts his case. He says that he is a devout practicing Presbyterian, and agrees with its message of following in footsteps of Christ. But he goes on to say:

Letters, K Apthorpe. The trouble is that the Churches are swimming against the tide. Most people from the Churches can see not dangers in forbidden fruit if they are swallowed sensibly, and reason that **if** excesses occur, **then** some action should be taken to help the sinners. **But all the pleasures should not be denied to all because a small few might fail.**

As it turned out, though, every year the messages described above fell on deaf ears. There is no hope of selling serious messages to Australians in the holiday season. In January, people are spread all over the land, the city has gone to the country and beaches, and the country has gone to the city and more beaches.

Their days are spent in having cups of tea and talking, or in playing Chinese Checkers or poker or pontoon. In the afternoons they watch tennis on the new TV, and later have a barbie and a beer or two that takes them into the evening. Among such a busy schedule, there is just no time for heavy talk about ethics and religion and loyalty to the flag. That must be saved for the long-away next month.

Comment. I wonder whether the New Year messages serve any useful public purpose at all. **I can remember** when Churchill and then Menzies declared war on Germany at the start of the war. **And then** Churchill and Curtin, still on the radio, celebrating its end. Since then, I can't **remember** a single message, never mind just New Year's greeting. Nor can I remember any one who was fortified by such. Still, **maybe** they **do** serve a useful purpose.

I'll leave you to decide. Next New Year's Day, when you open your newspaper or computer, have a look at the outpourings and ask whether they have any effect on you at all.

In any case, my period of self indulgence is over. The news-hounds have had their break and will soon fill the media with gritty stories and as much fear and loathing as they can generate. I will do my best not to do the same.

THE NEW INDONESIA

Prior to the war, a vast number of islands stretched from the Malayan and Singapore regions down to West New

Guinea. The Dutch had occupied these lands for a century and more, and extracted much wealth from them.

After the War, these islands suspected that the period of colonisation would now end, and that they could unite into a single nation, to be called Indonesia, and could drive out the Dutch and become independent.

By 1958, this process was well under way and a coherent nation had emerged. It was not easy for them because the Dutch were not keen to give up the assets and influence that they had built up over a century acquiring. So the process of their withdrawal was halting and the possiblity of real conflict was already just round the corner.

Australia did not officially get too much involved in this. There were however many vocal groups advocating all sorts of views. **One obvious group** said that all Asians were bad and treacherous and wanted somehow for them to go away. **Other groups** considered the new nation as a possible threat to our safety, and in particular thought that if it took over West New Guinea, then we were at even greater risk. **Many** proclaimed-Christians thought we should give them all the help we could, and some even said we should accept a token number as migrants. **The official Government line** was that it was not really our business, and that we should offer only advice at this stage.

The *SMH* got down to specifics. It had been printing stories of "**independence movements**" that were establishing in Indonesia for the purpose of **liberating West New Guinea**. These were private armies who were exercising on islands nearby, and whose vowed intention was to invade New Guinea and expel the Dutch. The Indonesian Government said that it had no control over these, and even made the silly claim that it had no knowledge of them. But they were real enough, and in later years they did make forays into New Guinea, though most of them were eaten by villagers. Still, their existence shows that **Indonesia was living on a knife edge.** Other armies in other provinces were also setting themselves up, and not all of them were friendly towards the central government.

At this stage, then, Indonesia was in a state of perilous instability, with all the problems of ousting the Dutch, of securing a centralised government in its stead, and with the haunting threat that the Reds there might be able to get a foothold during this period of uncertainty.

We will keep an eye of this festering situation as it develops over the months in the hope that it will not develop into any form of military confrontation with Australia.

THE CHURCHES AND GAMBLING

The Protestant Churches early in the month ran a campaign against the various forms of gambling that were springing up right across the nation and which the various State Governments appeared to be encouraging for the purpose of taxing the betting.

This was a period when all our Christian Churches were racked by sectarianism. First of all, the Protestants said and believed all sorts of unChristian-like things about Catholics, and the Catholics were likewise happy to respond in kind. Then, within the Protestants, despite some harmonious large scale gatherings, the **public petty point-scoring among clergy was a constant source of delight to non-believers.**

So when it came to the question of the bad influence that gambling was having, opinions were very divided. The Catholics mainly stayed out of the very large controversy that developed. One writer put the Catholic case succinctly. He said that gambling was not in itself bad, and that it was **only if were taken in excess** should it be considered so. If it came to the stage where it was affecting family income, or leading to crime, then it was an evil. But in most cases, this was not so, and the enjoyment that people got from it was not sinful but rather the legitimate celebration of an active life with beneficial interaction with the community.

This attitude did not satisfy everyone.

> **Letters, K N Lincoln.** At a time when some harmonious thinking with the Protestants was becoming evident, how disheartening it was to read of the usual negative attitude of the Roman Catholic Church on the jackpot tote question.
>
> A combined effort from all Churches could well prove very effective in an endeavour to lift this State from its all-time low in moral standing. But the Catholic dignitaries chose to stand aloof and not involve themselves in this latest encouragement to break the family bank.

The Protestants were left to carry on the battle by themselves. They did so on a number of fronts. They decried State Governments that relied on gambling revenue to balance their budgets. They abhorred the attitude of governments that did not attack the causes of gambling. These were seen to be shortage of housing, inequality of income, and insecurity caused by lack of health insurance. When these were coupled with boredom induced by living in a cycle of poverty with no way out, they necessarily encouraged gambling.

Then there were attacks based on the Bible. Much was said, **sometimes in context**, about the sin of covetousness, and gaining money by sloth, and even the sin of stealing got a mention. In most of these, the Letter ended with a quote from the Bible, as if this closed the deal and no more could be said on the subject. These arguments, needless to say, were mainly from Ministers of religion.

The argument spilled over onto the stock market. Surely the buying and selling of shares was a gamble. A few writers said the answer to this lay with the intentions of the buyer. If his intention was to seriously invest, then there was no problem. If he was just buying so that he could sell at an opportune date, then this was wrong. One writer suggested that potential buyers should thus have to answer in advance if they were buying as sinners or for true investment. Then, the sinners should be excluded from transactions.

The arguments got further and further from the issue. If a boy was climbing a tree, surely he was gambling that he would not fall and would return safely to earth again. One answer was that if he was climbing for apples that were not his, then he was gambling. If he was climbing for pleasure, then no gambling was involved.

The debate went on and on. This often happens in January because **all the news-hounds are on holidays** too, and the Editor needs any material at all to fill its pages.

In the long run, discussion was stifled by the various State Premiers saying, in one way or another, that they represented the people, and it was clear that the ordinary householder wanted a flutter now and then, and that the laws as they were would stand. In most cases, they went to imply that other forms of gambling would be introduced in the future and this would reduce the taxation burden that citizens would otherwise suffer.

Then, inevitably after such a rag-tag discussion, one writer popped up with the idea that this was what the churches professed to be doing all that time. That is, they took from the rich and gave to the poor. Most gamblers had extra money, and they donated, via betting and taxes, to help the poorer classes. Surely then gambling should be seen as fulfilling the very basics of the Christian faith.

MANHUNTS IN THE RICHER SUBURBS

Australia was a lot more prosperous that it had been twenty years ago. It was also becoming better educated, and parents were becoming more conscious that perhaps poverty did not have to be passed from generation to generation, but there could be a "**way out**". Of course, in the past, there had been dreams of fluking a greyhound dog, or becoming a champion boxer, or winning the lottery. But, now, much closer to reality, was the opportunity for all to **climb out of poverty by education**.

The idea that getting some sort of ticket, some type of certification, would raise you above the masses was taking hold. **The parents of baby boomers**, who had spent their lives in dead end jobs, wanted their children to do better that they had, and to move up a class or two. So courses for tradesmen, and typists, and lawyers and nurses, and doctors and teachers, and what have you, attracted large numbers of students, and the **new Commonwealth scholarships** and the new deal for apprentices helped the movement along.

But there were other ways out, other that studying. One of these, mostly but not exclusively reserved for girls, was to lie in wait for some innocent affluent male, and snap him up for a period of wedded bliss. The Letters below speak of this.

Letters, (Mrs) Margaret Hall. It would be a great relief to the parents of male aspirants to the Matriculation and Leaving Certificate and a gracious gesture if the fanatic "social mammas" of teenage daughters could call off the "manhunt" in all its forms and declare a closed season for at least the last term of the school year, so that their quarry could do some serious study. Home life is made a nightmare by the irruptions of persistent young females to whom land-mines and barbed wire would prove no deterrent.

Since the headmasters of leading schools gave way, under pressure, no doubt; and consented to school dances; silly and unnecessary functions, the whole thing has snowballed, and we have a plethora of "little dances," parties and Lord knows what else on any pretext.

As the mother of two boys in Leaving, I am appalled at the pernicious practice indulged in by a certain type of parent in launching children of school age into a synthetic social whirl where their sex instincts are aroused at too early an age, and they become pleasure-loving and spendthrift; when their proper sphere should be one of study and discipline and healthy, manly sports; not lolling around with the opposite sex.

It would seem we are well on the way to decadence before become civilised.

Letters, Margaret Champion. I am happy to say that I am a mother of three, an ex-doctor, and that all my children are now in universities at various levels.

Following various letters about the predatory nature of some mothers at senior school, I want to warn other mothers that the marriage market is indeed thriving at Sydney University.

In particular, there are bunches of girls, from the middle class in the Eastern suburbs and the North Shore, who take Arts and do something clever and elitist, like fencing, who are intelligent and attractive. Their sole aim at university is to lie in wait for some besotted successful young men with a future and tie the knot before they have a chance. The competition between them is fierce, and I can tell you that a doctor and a lawyer are much in demand though, for the more romantic, there is a good market for vets. Engineers are scarcely worth mentioning.

Comment to male readers. Be warned. If you are going off to University, watch out for these attractive young ladies with unworthy designs. If you are lucky and successful, you might get caught.

IS THE CIRCUS CRUEL?

Remember the circuses of the 1950's? Big tents, lots of animal smells, people in strange costumes, clowns, horses, elephants, lions and tigers and their trainers, monkeys, pretty girls in skimpy clothing, men and women of the trapeze. Sometimes a bearded lady, a snake charmer, a strong man, and a Ring Master in a top hat. A marvelous unreal world that came and went once a year to most big towns and suburbs.

But as we left the world of the Wild West, civilisation was creeping forward, and we started to realise that there might be some unhappy consequences to our love of the circus. These Letters below are early signs of the times to come.

Letters, (Miss) Isabella Ellis. It is to be hoped circuses will remain in outer areas and, through lack of support, ultimately disappear.

Most of their appeal depends on acts involving cruelty to wild animals, lions, tigers, and other large cats, which deprived of freedom and exercise, are trundled from place to place in cramped, insanitary cages to perform wearisome and undignified tasks for which whip and goad are effective educators.

But, for circus lovers, all was not lost.

Letters, Ian Westbrook. In reply to a letter alleging cruelty to circus animals. If you watch a circus performance closely you will see that "whips" and "goads" are used to give animals their cues, not to hit them with.

Horses and elephants have been domesticated for at least a thousand years, and are used to being tethered and mastered by man.

Lions in their natural state are thin and always hungry. In captivity they are well fed and are exercised in a big cage during the day and at performances. Incidentally, the cages are not insanitary but are scrubbed and cleaned out daily.

Once while doing a back country trip by road, one of Wirth's lorries drawing a lion's cage was overtaken by a motorist. He told the driver that a lion had been running behind the cage for the last mile or so. The attendant got out, swung the unfastened door open, and the lion jumped in. Obviously it preferred the comfort and food of the circus to the uncertainty of freedom.

Comment. I miss the lion-tamers of the 1950's. There was always the dreadful but thrilling thought that a few of the lions would revert to nature and eat their host. As well as that, some of the other measures of animal welfare have reduced the excitement of the Big Top. So, I miss those great circuses, but I know their days have gone. But I shall not complain. What a pity that we can't always have the best of both worlds.

NEWS AND VIEWS

A lad in Sydney climbed on to the top of a Wirth's Circus cage and **started feeding a lion**. He put his arm into the cage, and **the lion bit it off**. The lad survived.

Things in Indonesia are hotting up. Armed rebels took over the oilfields in Sumatra, and a few days later were subdued by Government forces in pitched military battles.

Lazy Aussies. Sydney's Water Board has decided that automatic flushing of urinals in public lavatories will be banned. Such flushing is generally used in men's toilets to remove smells and perhaps health risks....

Supporters of automatic flushing say that the "average Australian is too lazy or dubious to pull the chain", so it should be done for him.

Letters, Ernest Fisk. One of your news headlines on August 13 employs a new phrase which, presumably, originated recently in North America, viz.: "Missile Detonated on the Edge of Space."

I, and probably other readers, would feel grateful if you could tell us **where is "The Edge of Space"?**

FEBRUARY NEWS ITEMS

An American cruise-ship, *SS Lurline*, arrived in Sydney, and was greeted with fan-fare at the docks. This was the **first US passenger liner to visit since the war**, and hopefully it will be the vanguard to guide tourists here in the future.

Sydney's Bondi Beach is having trouble with people **dropping rubbish near the beach.** Most of it is **newspapers used as wrapping for fish and chips.** Fourteen people were warned by the ranger in one day, and the Council has warned that they will be fined a minimum of five Pounds in future. The Council will employ a full-time ranger to police the near-surf area.

January 2nd. The United States Army has put a Vanguard satellite into space. But it is a bit of a disappointment for backyard viewers because it is not as big as the Russian sputniks and will be seen only at dusk and sunset on many fewer days. It shows, though, that the **US is still well and truly in the space race.**

The Queen Mother, Mary, will visit Australia soon. She will be **given a brooch** by the Government. It will be over three inches long, using a hibiscus as a motif, and will contain 364 diamonds form South Africa, and 34 rubies from Burma. **It will be valued at 5,000 Pounds.** This is about five times the average salary of a middle-class worker.

February 6th. The **US Army** launched its own Vanguard satellite on last Friday. This Wednesday, **the US Navy** tried to launch its a similar rocket into space, but it exploded after 60 seconds in flight. No reason has yet been found.

A national Health Conference decided that **the link between smoking and cancer was "sinister"**, and noted that heavy smoking increased the risk of cancer many-fold. It will seek ways to make this known to smokers....

Comment. This link was apparent to many in the scientific community, but generally **it was news to most citizens**, and smoking continued to increase for decades. Part of the reason was that the greater appeal of cigarettes over the "filthy habit" of **roll-your-own**.

Times were tough for publicans, after decades of mind-blowing profiteering and arrogance. The average pub was losing 70 Pounds a week to the new clubs that were springing up....

A ULVA report recommended that seats be provided in bars for customers, and that they should strive for cleaner, quieter hotels. "**The publican should be presented as a family man, a church-goer, and a citizen with public interests**". **Comment.** For the pubs, and the publican, those changes would take some doing.

February 15th. The Queen Mother arrived in Canberra, and was greeted enthusiastically by a crowd of 2,000, many of them school children with the day off from school.

Of interest: During her drive across Canberra, she changed vehicles. She went from **a landaulette** to an open car. Of course you do not need me to tell you what a landaulette is.

LASSETER'S GOLD

In Early February, the *SMH* ran an article by a geologist that was highly critical of the business-man and explorer L H Lasseter. This latter gentleman was inspired by the dream that there was a vast reef of gold somewhere near the Simpson Desert in Western Australia. In 1930, he organised finance for a search, and led a team of half a dozen men towards the Simpson. Team members gradually dropped out, and Lasseter was left to die alone in the desert.

The writer of the article cast considerable doubts on the character of Lasseter, and on the existence of the reef. A few days after the article was printed, the following Letter, **from his son**, was published in defence of the man.

Letters, R Lasseter. I bitterly resent the numerous articles published recently about my dead father, L H Lasseter, and especially take exception to your article "Why Not End the Fable of Lasseter's Gold?"

The writer's accusations of my father's "lack of balance and excessive imagination" is defamation of character and is most unjustified, as I have numerous personal references, letters and other papers bearing testimony to his good character and sane thinking, and his statement that my father "died of his own free will" is as callous and brutal as it is untrue.

His battle for survival and terrible death during the 78 days after his food ran out is, in fact, further testimony to his courage and determination to win through against severe odds and, even under these conditions, he retained his sanity when many others would have lost their reason.

Everyone is entitled to his opinion as to whether Lasseter's Reef exists, but that does not give people the right to defame a man whose solid convictions do not agree with their own ideas. He certainly believed in his reef; even Terry agrees with this. How then can anyone blame him for the "public and private money" which Terry claims has been "poured down the drain" to glorify his name.

He cannot be blamed that his name has become well known and that the area has been called "Lasseter Country," to the apparent jealous distaste of your writer. If the inland bushmen have been "riled" as Terry states by the country being called "Lasseter Country" then who gave it that name? Certainly not Lasseter or his relations.

"Noted Explorer" Terry would be well advised to seek fame from his own exploration work rather than by discrediting the efforts of another man.

Let me make it clear that at the moment I am expressly defending the man - his personal qualities and reputation. I am not discussing any pros and cons relating to the reef.

The reported words of Bob Buck most aptly sum up my own feelings - "Why can't they let the poor flaming cow rest in peace."

Comment. To date, no gold reef has been discovered despite many expeditions that have sought it.

It seems though, that some of our other explorers were not treated kindly, even in school text-books.

Letters, Rosemary Howe. I most sincerely feel for Lasseter in his letter regarding the lamentable way his father's name has been abused.

In my own case, I have shared with my family the indignation arising from publications about the explorer Captain William Hilton Hovell and his colleague Hamilton Hume. Even Hovell's name is mispronounced as "hovel," this being ironical, as the name is derived from "Hautville" (high house).

However, my real concern is that in schools throughout Australia, it is taught that these two men violently quarrelled on their historic overland trip to Port Phillip, when in fact no quarrel arose until many years later.

A recent book, "Our First Overlander," is being used in schools to perpetuate this nonsense. No mention is made of the other explorations by Hovell, nor the fact that he died disregarded and largely unrewarded for his efforts.

Hovell was my great-grandfather, and I join with Mr Lasseter in hoping that facts and not conjecture are used about our pioneers.

WHINGING POMS

Since the War ended, almost a million migrants have entered this country. Most of these were from Britain, and most came on some form of assisted passage. That means that they would be offered some help in finding jobs and accommodation, and in return they would be contracted to stay for three years. Some of the families that took up this offer regarded it as a working holiday, and planned to go back home in three years. Others planned to do this, but found life here attractive, and settled in as permanents.

Some others did not like much of Australia at all, and went back to Mother England. Among these, quite a few put pen to paper and explained just why they did this. Now and then, they touched raw nerves in this nation, and then Letters flooded in telling of the many sides to this issue.

The excerpts below from a "whinging Pom" started this particular ball rolling.

Letters, Ralph Rowlatt. Mr Tiptaft, ex-Lord Mayor of Birmingham, is reported as saying that his most powerful impression during a visit here is that British immigrants are not told the whole truth about Australia before they sail.

He is right. Official migration literature is silent about a vast number of unfavourable matters. When I arrived I was appalled by such things as the incredible amount of rubbish, beer bottles (often broken) and spittle that fouls the streets and public spaces; the immature vulgarity that fills so much of the popular newspapers, magazines and commercial broadcasting; the crude and ill-mannered advertising plastered over buildings everywhere; the suburban "roads" without sealing, gutters and kerbs.

Later I was to be dismayed by the abundance of public houses and the scarcity of public libraries; the impossibility (and even now, the difficulty) of getting a housing loan on reasonable terms; the veritable disease of gambling; and the marked absence of religion, with the inevitable consequences of the absence of a sense of social responsibility, a concentration on things material to the neglect of things mental and spiritual, and the low status accorded to women.

Like many other British migrants, I came out chiefly for the sake of the children, but I soon understood why so many return, or would like to return, for the same reason.

The early responses are shown below.

Letters, Leslie Ball. Mr Ralph Rowlatt is quite definite that potential British migrants are not told the truth about conditions here prior to leaving, and it appears that once having arrived, he is appalled.

I am rapidly coming to the conclusion that of all the hundreds of thousands of British migrants who have arrived since the war, *I was the only one who was told all the facts before I sailed. This, of course, is quite ridiculous* - there is nothing special about me - I was just another Englishman with a young family who saw in Australia the chance for progress that Britain (at least in 1951) didn't seem to be able to offer.

It was made very clear to me (long before I decided to migrate) what conditions were like in hostels and emergency housing centres, and, in fact, I was shown photographs of Bradfield and Hargrave Parks. Incidentally I spent almost three years in these centres, and, contrary to popular belief, they are not entirely populated by "no-hopers". I apologise if I offend Mr Rowlatt's aesthetic susceptibilities by using that well-known Australianism.

Mr Rowlatt has, of course, made the same mistake as that made by the people who write regularly to the editors of daily newspapers and sign themselves "Misled Pommy". That is, the mistake of comparison. Ask any migrant what he came to Australia for, and if he is truthful, he will say "A fresh start." **The fresh start is doomed to failure if there is a constant comparison with conditions in England.**

Surely Mr Rowlatt is not allowing his outlook to be clouded by the less-desirable aspects of life in Australia. Every nation has its problems but for my part, the many "pubs", beer bottles, ill-mannered advertising, and so on, doesn't make the slightest difference to my way of life.

Why not look at the good things this country has to offer, Mr Rowlatt. They **are** there, you know.

Letters, R W Miller. Are we, or is Australia, as bad as they say? No doubt some of the things they say about us are true, but I feel that Mr Rowlatt is overcritical of conditions here, and he will obviously never be happy here. He is one of those people who should never have come here in the first place.

I suspect - in fact, I have been led to believe - that some of the things he complained of are to be found also in England and elsewhere. While we no doubt have our faults, and have not many amenities to be found in more closely populated areas, it should be remembered that we are a young country, and it is only by increasing our population that many of the missing amenities can be provided.

Then there followed **a spate of defensive Letters** that criticised things in Britain. A typical such Letter is given below.

Letters, D Cooper. I believe that upwards of 50 per cent of the housing in cities such as Liverpool and Salford (to name but two) is considered virtually unfit for human habitation, yet the present occupants have no prospect of getting better accommodation in the near future. In addition, these cities, where row upon row of terraced dwellings abut straight on to the street, are cursed with a degree of atmospheric pollution the like of which Sydney has never known: dust and soot are deposited from the atmosphere at the rate of 600 tons per square mile per year.

The standard of journalism varies from the sublime (e.g., "The Times," "Manchester Guardian") to the deplorable, of which examples are too many to mention.

The average English working man has **two** abiding passions. **The first** is his regular drink at the "local"; the criticism that is usually levelled at Australia in this respect is that "pub-life," as known in England, does not exist here. In this light, Mr Rowlatt's complaint about the abundance of public houses in Australia rings rather hollow. **The second passion** is the weekly football pool. The pools organisation is such that, when the English Soccer season ends in April, the pools continue to run on the results of matches played where? In Australia!

So far as the low status of women is concerned, take the time-worn example. An Englishman rarely offers to surrender his seat in a train or bus to a lady. I have even seen pregnant women allowed to stand for quite long distances in a jolting bus.

After that, the knives were out. The weather, the monarchy, the class system, the pubs, their sports, their pale colour and lack of sunshine, the political parties, their lack of space, their school system and their washing habits. All of these, and others, got mentions that were not favourable.

But, mind you, none of these answered the charges against Australia directly. Britain, they said, suffered by comparison, but they scarcely spoke about Australia.

A few days later, more considered Letters appeared.

Letters, (Mrs) Lotte Bentley. Mr Rowlatt, in his criticism, seems to be like the man who still believes in the beautiful "blue" Danube in the country of my origin, Austria. Perhaps, with a little goodwill, he will in time, be able to realise that beneath the surface of the very human failures he lists so despairingly, there rests **the golden heart of the Australian**.

Nowhere since my birth in Yugoslavia, residence in Austria and short stay in England and the Far East, have I met friendlier people than here. Why not try to get to know them and love them for what they are? That would be a contribution to "things spiritual and mental" to the neglect of things material. As a mother, I think there is no environment more conducive to a full development of children than in this country.

I should venture to say that there is as much religion here as anywhere in the old countries, and as for the disease of gambling, I suspect no (immigration) pamphlet would advertise a human vice as old as the human race as one of a country's attractions, be it football, horses or dogs; it seems fairly universally spread among humanity.

This opened the way for comments on the people of Oz.

Letters, G E Verbeek. As for the Australian people not being religious, I think, person for person, they compare favourably with other nationalities. Whether they are religious or not, I can honestly say they are the kindest and most warm-hearted people in the world, always ready to come to the help of anyone in distress. Surely kind hearts are more than coronets and come from religious feelings.

Letters, Viljen Puntervold. Most critiques I have read, written by overseas people, have always been based upon what they experienced and came up against - social or otherwise - in the cities or close by. Few, if any, wander out into **the real Australia, which is the open station country and the farm lands**, the small townships and hamlets, as well as the desert and timber regions.

The rural and seafaring population of the old world who come here rarely condemn or growl. They know better. They soon discover that here not only can they earn a good living, but enjoy an easy and fluent way of life compared with where they came from.

The professional type and the industrial workers are mainly concerned with what material gain they can accrue as quickly as possible in order to retire, either back to where they came from, or else where they believe they can live at ease.

They never seem to realise that Australia possesses a wonderful talisman; it is a country in which it is possible to grow and develop, where their children have a chance of permanent economic security. In short, here are all the main essentials for a happy way of life.

We hear a lot about the lack of culture in Australia. I wonder if the percentage of cultured people in Britain exceeds that of Australia? I doubt it. Isn't it a fact that as young as Australia is, she has nevertheless furnished some very valuable additions to the worlds of science, the fine arts, literature, etc?

I think the crux of the matter is this: An overseas person either takes to Australia like a duck to water or else he or she will never feel at home here at all, which in the latter case can only be remedied by leaving and trying somewhere else.

The discussion did not end there. It still goes on. It also affects other areas of life. Is Rugby League better than Union? Is Melbourne better that Sydney? Is Town better that Country? Are greyhounds better to watch than horses? Such disputes are inevitable. Most people make their minds up early, and most of these never change.

In the above Letters, I think that Australians at the time were conscious that we were backward in some matters, and over the years we have corrected many of them. But for some of them, **it was debatable whether we needed correction.** For example, local English pubs are great, but do they fit into Australia with its big distances and many clubs? Then there is the argument that we do not need more religion, but rather less. Do we want very elitist education and social systems?

I suspect that it all comes down to personal preference and to the amount of national resources that the nation can find to make gradual changes when we somehow decide to make them.

But, probably I am wrong. **What do you think?**

THE ROYAL VISIT

The arrival of the Queen Mother, Mary, was hailed throughout the nation. The tour was a great success, with all the normal ceremonies, processions, balls, banquets, and crowds. The most over-used words in the Press were "informal" and "charming". Mary had some hard days in the heat of our summer, often without umbrellas, and wore it all with good grace.

A few writers had their grouches. One source of complaint was the gift of the expensive brooch to Mary.

Letters, M Harrison. So another Royal lady is to be presented with another diamond brooch.

I only hope her Majesty will not think the Australian people are as one-track minded as the Prime Minister. Would not a nice **opal** bracelet or dress ring be more appropriate for the occasion, something really Australian? Why must Mr Menzies insist on presenting the Queens of England with diamonds when they already have more than they can wear? An ordinary schoolgirl could have made a better choice.

Letters, Kathleen Jensen.

I venture to suggest that it would have been more appropriate to present the Queen Mother with **a cheque** to give to crippled children's organisations in Australia, or to a fund for aged people, not to mention the need for an endowment for cancer research.

One feels that the Queen Mother would appreciate such a gesture rather than have what is really only another item to add to her already extensive collection of jewellery.

Letters, T Barker. I should like to thank M Harrison, who expresses the opinions of so many Australians that **our lovely opals** are discarded and imported gems chosen as gifts to visiting Royalty.

We do not hear of any opals in the collection of Royal jewels. One wonders why?

Though one writer did support the more conventional approach.

Letters, H. Walter. Your correspondent Mrs Kathleen Jensen suggests that a cheque to be presented to the Queen Mother to give to charitable organisations would have been more suitable than a valuable piece of jewellery.

Despite the fact that the Queen Mother has an extensive collection of jewellery, the spirit of democracy in which this gift is presented by Australia is something to be proud of, as a token is always a memorial to awaken memory in years to come.

Another source of the complaint was "hardships" felt by children who attended the parades. Note that VAD's were volunteers who provided assistance to the more military groups in times of war and national emergency.

Letters, David Carlton. My daughter was on parade last Saturday in the Epping VAD squad. Now for facts: She got up about 6 a.m. and ironed her uniform (she was ordered it had to be immaculate). From home she stood in the bus to the railway station at Beecroft (she left the house at 7.55 a.m.). She stood in the train to Wynyard.

She marched to Government House, and stood at attention for a long and quite unnecessary time. You reported 30 Servicewomen fainted. Fifty or more Servicewomen fainted.

Now these VADs were told they must not stir or their dresses would be crushed. No consideration was made as to how far and how long these girls travelled. I know the Queen Mother would be shocked if she knew what goes on.

But others saw this situation differently.

Letters, Ralph Bindley. The letter from David Carlton gave details of the tribulations of his daughter, who attended the parade. May I comment upon them?

Firstly, she could have ironed her shirt the night before. **Secondly, everyone** stands in public transport to avoid crushing their clothes. She in not special.

Thirdly, of course she walked to Government House. How else would she get there.

Fourthly, Mr Carlton wants to know if the Queen Mother "knows what goes on." **Of course she does**.

Her Majesty knows exactly "what goes on." She knows full well with what zeal and enthusiasm these parades are entered upon. She knows exactly how much work and preparation are necessary. She knows, too, in the case of the VADs, it is a Labor of love, and that they do it in their own time, not for the glamour, but with pride in their units and in Saturday's parade - out of love, loyalty and affection for a Queen Mother who fully appreciates their efforts.

Comment. Despite such inevitable grizzles, the tour was a grand spectacle throughout. It once again reinforced the fact that **the Royal Family was still a symbol of significance**, and that we as a nation were still mightily attached to Britain and the Empire.

MARCH NEWS ITEMS

Remember Dr Vivian Fuchs who was **racing neck-and-neck towards that South Pole** with Edmund Hillary? Well, he is still in the news because he has now completed his longer journey to traverse the Antarctic from the Weddell Sea to the Ross Sea. He and his nine-man team were the first men to complete this feat....

It took 99 days, and covered 2,100 miles, an enormous distance, when you think about it. He will receive a knighthood from the Queen. **Part of his celebration included having a hot bath.**

Polio was a disease that was crippling many people, often the very young. A startling new report from three eminent doctors in London said that **a boy was bitten by a budgerigar** that was affected by polio. He died soon after from polio, and they made the assumption that the bird's polio had been transmitted to the boy....

This statement was at variance with the popular conception that the disease was not transferable from animals to humans. It caused much concern at the time, but was **later judged to be wrong**.

Key Money hit the headlines. **This was a racket** that resulted from government control of rents. This control was part of war-time regulations that were still in place in NSW and Victoria and froze rents at 1941 levels. This in itself was a racket that **captured votes from renters**, as opposed to the many fewer landlords....

Renters were almost impossible to move out. When they did, the landlord could get new tenants and raise the rent. **So the racket was to pay existing tenants money to leave. It was illegal to do this blatantly**, so instead the landlords paid for the key to the premises. There was no law preventing trading in keys, and so access could be gained for a new tenant at a much higher rental....

The sums involved often reached over 1,000 Pounds. One landlord was sent **to gaol for four months for accepting key money.** This rort had been obvious for too long. Is it now time to change the Landlord and Tenant Act? The answer was "maybe". In NSW, it took ten years before all the necessary changes were made.

Grace Kelly was a well-known American actress, and married Prince Rainier, of Monaco, in 1956. **She has given birth to her second child....**

In 1919, an agreement was signed with France that said that **if the Prince died without a male heir**, Monaco would revert to France. That would mean that its 20,000 inhabitants would have to pay income tax, and they would be **liable to fight in the French army**....

Her first child was a girl. Needless to say, **the arrival of a boy was greeted with joy by Monaco's citizens.**

Private Elvis Presley is now in the Army. Every move he makes is featured on TV, with the connivance of the publicity-hungry Army. **Thousands of girls wrote to ask for a lock of his hair** when he got his military haircut. Sadly, the logistics involved were too much, and they were disappointed.

BREAD HANDLING

Letters, Anne McDougall. Now that the Government seems to be displaying some zeal for reform, would it give a thought to the condition in which bread is served to the public? Bread is handled in the course of its delivery by half a dozen hands whose cleanliness is open to doubt. It is also subject to certain vicissitudes in the course of delivery, which I have myself witnessed.

It stands on open counters in shops, and is patronised by the flies. It is handled by the same pair of hands that deals out your change. I have seen a dozen loaves spilled out on the roadway and gathered up after a dusting off, and delivered. I have also seen the driver in the course of his deliveries pawing though a heap of garbage on the roadside.

RAMBLING THOUGHTS ON BREAD

The above Letter reminded me of the various rules that have come and gone in the delivery of all goods, including bread. Let me go back to the zoning laws as they were in 1958, and let me ramble about a little while I think of them.

Zoning of bread deliveries to homes was introduced during the War. This meant that a baker could only deliver to a prescribed number of houses, and that he could not deliver to anyone else, and no one else could come on to his patch. This was designed to cut down on duplication of wasteful services.

Many housewives did not like this, because some bakers became arrogant and others did not measure up. A few years ago, the NSW government removed zoning, but bakers liked their strangle-hold on delivery, so they set up an elaborate system to beat the new rules.

For example, they agreed among themselves that if a housewife wanted bread from a second baker, the first one would deliver it and pretend that it had been made by the first baker, and that he was just the deliverer. Clearly, this frustrated housewives and the purpose of the law.

The Government now came up with a new law that said all bakers would be given a unique number, and that number would have to be included in the cooking process and displayed on the side of the finished loaves. That way, a housewife would know which baker was responsible for the baking of it.

The result was that each loaf of bread, and each half loaf, came with a largish five-digit number imprinted into its side. This put an end to one more rort in the home delivery industry. Of course, in general, this industry was getting close to death anyway. Within a few years, it had gone completely. Until then, you could get ice, bread, fruit and vegetables, rabbits, eggs, milk, clothes props, insurance policies, all delivered to your door.

Before the War, many of these came with the assistance of a horse and dray. In any case, with the growth of larger shops, then shopping chains, then supermarkets, home deliveries have died out until a resurgence in the last few years. In the baking industry, larger corporations took-over small local bakers, and bread in wrapping paper, and sliced bread, became popular. Different standards of hygiene were gradually implemented, and the idea of bread coming in a basket and being "halved" by the delivery-man's bare hands became untenable.

Comment. These brief musings on the progress of the bread industry could be repeated for all consumer products for the home. Though changes at the time seemed slow, and it might have appeared that improvements always lagged, never the less various systems did alter incrementally, and I think it true to say that the method of getting a product like bread, from producer to the home, has changed out of sight.

SCHOOL MILK

I find that if I gather oldies into discussion groups, and let them talk about the golden days of their childhood, they initially find common ground with memories of Saturday arvo at the pictures, and follow up with descriptions of the free milk that was delivered to schools. Here, I will meander again down memory lane, and meditate on school milk. To get the discussion going, I will start with this little Letter below.

> **Letters, B B Smyth.** Recently when at a friend's home, I was shocked at the child's reply to her mother's question: Did she drink her issue of school milk? The child (aged 8) said there was none left for her; "the big girls got it today."
>
> I asked two girls attending the same school (one aged 12 and the other 9) if each child was given a bottle of milk daily. The elder child said: "Oh no! It is put on a table and you take what you want. I had three bottles of milk today."

By the time WWII was nearing its end, the delivery of free milk to schools was well established. Different States had their own ways of doing this, but what they had in common was that about half a pint of unhomogenised milk was brought to supposedly every primary school in Australia for consumption by the pupils. The idea was that milk was essential to the young, and that war-time uncertainties and shortages meant that some children were missing out, or not getting enough on a regular basis. Our young citizens were thus moved to the top of the priority list.

One personal correspondent remembered his experience. He wrote:

> In the first two years, a big churn of milk was left at the gate of the school. Four boys from sixth class were sent to get it for play-time, and they left it outside in the sun. In the first term, it was a heavy churn, so they spilled most of it half the time. At play time, one of the nuns ladled it out into china cups that every child might or might not have, and anyone who wanted it could have a drink.
>
> Quickly, the novelty wore off, and no one turned up to get their quota. So it was made mandatory for all to partake. This was unpopular, since the milk was always heavy with cream, it was often on the turn, and queueing up to get it took up all play-time. This latter objection resulted in the distribution time being moved to lunch-time, and by then it was definitely curdled, and full of lumps. It became more unpopular.
>
> Over the next year, buyer resistance grew to one hundred percent. Then, technology changed everyone's attitude. Milk was delivered in small bottles, with round cardboard lids. This was extremely popular with the boys because they developed various gambling games, and the winners were paid in lids. In a school where there was no hint of money, the boy with the biggest pile of lids was king of the castle.
>
> The milk, when it was delivered to the school, came with a quarter of a block of ice. This was good for crushing and putting down the back of shirts. That

was generally a good use for it, but in Summer it had all melted by the time we got to school, so for those months, it was not much use to anyone.

As for the milk, it never came back into favour. A few times we were forced by the good nuns to drink it "because if we do not drink it, we will lose it." But after a few sessions of mass vomiting, it was decided that compulsion was not a solution.

I have found over the years that this Letter is fairly typical. Its effects were not just felt in the schools. For example, a few milk-bar owners were fined for purloining crates of full bottles from outside schools before the students got there. Then there was the question of what happened in school holidays. There was no milk delivered. Did that mean children no longer needed the milk?

The people delivering the milk always wanted more pay. So milk deliveries were often cancelled because of strikes. When there was drought in an area, deliveries dried up. There were a few Letters demanding that at city schools where the milk was actually drunk, the **girls got the milk first so that they could later be sturdy enough to bear children**. At the same time, the dairy industry, and the bureaucracy behind the scheme, were all staunch supporters so that politics was always loitering.

Comment. I wonder what benefits the school milk programme delivered. I have had a bit of a look at what was available at the time, and found nothing other than blurbs from vested interests. From my own experience, and that of a lot of oldies, I would say no benefit at all. But I do not expect that to be the entire story. Maybe you can enlighten me with your own experiences.

KILLING DOGS

Over the last month, the RSPCA in NSW had obviously been disturbed. This worthy society to protect animals normally went about its business without fanfare and out of the public gaze, but recently it had found itself in the headlines as first one senior executive resigned, and then another. The public was not informed why this had occurred but leaks here and there indicated that a major problem was brewing.

In mid-March it all blew up. It seems that the public in NSW was being encouraged to turn in lost dogs to the Society. Most people who did this expected that good homes would be found for the dogs. Some of the more knowledgeable knew that the dogs would be destroyed, but thought they would still be better off than being homeless and roaming the streets to the distress of everyone.

What now became apparent was that many dogs were indeed being killed, but beyond that, they were being placed in chambers and gassed.

The public were shocked. Gas chambers had all too recently been the way that the Nazis had murdered the Jews and others, and the horror of those executions were still fresh in memories. It turned out that other States had done this in the past, but NSW was the only State that was still doing it.

Letters, Peter Thompson. I was sickened and disgusted when I read your report of the RSPCA's gas chamber, and think that it must be one of the most disgusting things revealed in Australia since the days of the massacres of the Aborigines.

It is incredible that such agony must be endured by these wretched animals, when so many more humane methods of killing them are within easy reach.

If the society cannot afford barbiturates, they could use clubs or knives, both of which are fast and relatively humane (and not so hard on the pocket as coal gas).

I am filled with remorse when I think of a very faithful dachshund bitch which was dying of a fatal bowel complaint and which I innocently imagined I was putting to a kind and painless death when I sent her to the society to be destroyed. I think I could have killed her more humanely with my own hands.

The conversation spread to the wider question of the problem of surplus dogs.

Letters, A L Eather. Dogs destroyed at the King Edward Dogs' Home are not all unwanted. Many are loved pets which have strayed and not been traced by their owners.

Thousands of dogs would be saved from the gas chamber if owners would put a disc on their dog's collar bearing name and address or phone number.

In South Australia and Northern Territory, this is compulsory and discs are issued with registrations.

Letters, B G Studdert. The killing of 10,000 dogs annually, in Sydney alone, makes unpleasant reading. But most of those dogs would never have been born if owners of female dogs (which make the best pets) would care for them properly or have them de-sexed.

The largest contributor to the menace and cruelty of the stray-dog problem are parents who buy or are given a "dear little puppy" for their children to play with. In many cases, when the animal grows up, it becomes a nuisance through lack of training and is turned out into the streets.

Letters, R S Jackson. I agree with Mr W. R. Lawrence, MLA, and his supporters that it was right to abolish the gas chamber and institute a more humane method of killing dogs, but it appears that the gas chamber has been in operation for many years without much objection from the members or the public.

Why wreck this great society because of this difference of opinion now? Would it not be better to call a general meeting of all members and have the propositions fairly before them, and if necessary have a council elected that would carry out the wishes of the majority.

It is easy to destroy but it is more difficult to build. The action of resigning from an organisation, because of the rejection of a point of view, is not the just solution of a problem.

Letters, R. Cunningham. It is indeed a pity that a great society like the RSPCA is bogged down with work caused by the indiscriminate breeding of dogs when there are greater and far more important matters for it to deal with.

In my opinion, the State Government could assist the society in its great work by requiring all dog breeders to become registered and by raising the licence fee from its present nominal amount to somewhere about 5 Pounds per annum.

This increased licence fee would reduce by about 70 per cent the number of parents buying a "little puppy dog" (all potential nuisances) to satisfy the whims of their children. Only people really desirous of having a good quality thoroughbred dog would not mind paying up.

Comment. The NSW Branch of the RSPCA decided soon after this that its gas chamber would be closed. After that, however, the problem with unwanted dogs continued unabated, and it remained one of the main causes of Letters at least until I finish this series of books in 1968.

COUNTRY AND EASTER SHOWS

Every year, right round Australia, in all small and all big cities, the farmers and graziers and wine makers and orchid growers and goat-cheese maker, and a host of others, like to put their best product on display for the world to see. So that Shows become important events in the country, as well as in the cities where the biggest and best produce is judged. These shows were important in 1958 not only for perpetuating interest in matters agricultural, but promoting the social life of remote communities that depend on such events as a focal point in what might otherwise become a dreary life.

The Sydney Show is, to coin a phrase, a show-stopper, and goes on for about 10 days, most days and most nights, before and during Easter. In 1958, it got close to a million visitors, and sold almost one million meat pies. It was not at all conspicuous for its depravity, indeed many held it to be proof that wholesome interests could satisfy people of all ages and sizes.

Because the show was held at Easter, it ran into flack from some writers who wanted this period to be sacred.

Letters, John M Felts. Good Friday is a day to be observed and not celebrated. It is observed by Christians as a day of solemn prayer and remembrance of the agony Christ went through for us. It is the day in which the blackest crime in the history of mankind was committed.

All this is forgotten by the general public due to the usual distractions that go with all public holidays.

Gay festivities, drunkenness, and the mad rush to the seaside and the country, all of these bring delight. The real meaning of it is pushed so far into the background that many people do not even know what it is supposed to represent.

I came from Florida and in that State, it is not a public holiday. This makes a world of difference in the way it is observed.

I think Good Friday should be observed in the same spirit that Remembrance Day was observed last November 11.

Letters, C O Plunkett. On the death of a demi-semi VIP down comes the flag to half-mast, so surely on the one Friday, during the few sad hours commemorating the finish of the earthly sojourn of the Most Important Person of all time, **flags should be lowered**.

Always on Good Friday in most American cities can be seen numerous half-masted flags and it is known that London will, for the first time, do likewise this year. Let us be with our mother city in this simple Christian act.

Then, turning to the Show, there were always others who argued specifically that the Show should close on Easter Friday. This year though, there was an extra Letter writer who suggested a compromise.

Letters, Denis Logan. The churches are again protesting about the opening of the RAS Show on Good Friday.

Would not all consciences be satisfied if the Friday program were to include some sort of religious ceremony? After all, the Show is in the nature of a harvest festival.

But, no. This was not to be. The churches are again protesting about the opening of the RAS Show on Good Friday.

Letters, David Conolly. Mr Denis Logan's letter simply shows how little acquainted he is with the events in the Church's year. "After all," he says, "the Show is in the nature of a harvest festival."

What kind of argument is that? Of all the days in the year, Good Friday is the last on which the church would ever hold a harvest festival.

It is also worth mentioning that Christians, in the true sense of the word, have never been satisfied with the kind of "tit-bit" Mr Logan suggests the Royal Agricultural Society should throw to them.

The suggestion he gave was that "some sort of religious ceremony" should be included with the other Showground activities on that day. Having got that rather tiresome moral duty over and done with, is the inference, we can really have the time of our lives while we desecrate what is sacred and precious to millions throughout the world.

But there was yet another view, and this would have riled both of the above writers.

Letters, A Reader. In view of the time, expense, energy and devotion which have been given to the preparation of the Royal Show, is it not time it remained open for the whole weekend?

As thousands want to see it and a crush develops on the public holidays, the Show should be open on Sundays as well. This would give family groups better chances of seeing the exhibits in more comfort.

Comment. This last writer got his way as more and more people moved further away from the idea of a sanctified Sunday. In the long run, the Sydney Show opened its gates on Sundays, but in a show of compromise, it closed them at dusk.

A NOTE ON SPORTSMANSHIP

Letters, H E Ellen. It is high time that steps were taken to eliminate from tennis the gamesmanship, prima donna-like displays of bad temper, and persistent arguments with umpires.

Umpires should be empowered to deal drastically with objectionable behaviour, as in the case of football.

If the tennis player who misbehaves was liable to be required to forfeit his match, or to submit to a period of suspension, there would be few spoilt prima donnas on the courts.

Comment. Some things never change.

ASSIMULATION OF ABORIGINES

Letters, Michael Sawtell. The news that the charming young full-blood Aboriginal girl Ruth Daylight, who was presented to the Queen Mother, is now living in a blacks' humpy at Halls Creek, Western Australia, does not surprise me in the least. That is the Aborigines' traditional way of living. **They have no housing sense.**

Last year I saw Albert Namatjira, the world-famous landscape artist, sitting in the bed of creek with Mrs Albert and the refrigerator on the bank out in the sun not being used.

It sounds well as sentimental publicity that a full-blood girl is presented to the Queen Mother, but the actual result is disastrous. **That girl's life, with the best of intentions, has been uprooted and spoilt.** She now lives in two worlds, and how is she to adjust her life?

Let us be sensible about these unfortunate Aboriginal girls and **keep them away from our white civilisation as far as possible and as long as possible.**

Letters, J Horner. Mr Michael Sawtell's letter advising us to leave "these unfortunate (black) girls and keep them away from our white civilisation as far as possible and as long as possible" is unintentionally sentimental. **He expects a policy of segregation to work.** Segregation has failed in Alabama, in Kenya, and in the West Indies, because it offers no ideas but racial tension. Only in Ghana, which is completely African country, is a commonsense racial segregation policy possible.

Let us be realistic about the Aborigines. They are facing their first radical social change in hundreds of years, and we are doing them no service by pretending that this urge for readjustment does not exist. But it is we who have the legislative and social initiative to help them make this change. There are no easy answers to this great problem.

In the very interesting case of Ruth Daylight, it is certainly wrong to take any child away from her parents. But this is not Mr Sawtell's objection. I think it is reasonable to interpret his letter, as well as Mr Paul Hasluck's statement in Canberra, **as deploring any social contact with white people that she may have made.** She may become restless, and even forget that it is the lot of a coloured person to live in poverty and frustration.

The official fear that she will pine away if taken "from her environment" rests on the sure knowledge that she will never fit into our society. But this is precisely where so much human wastage persists. We make more provision for these cases in New Guinea than we do for our own people.

Segregation is a mental dead-end. The recently written general principles of the Federal Council for Aboriginal Advancement lay down ideas for social integration of the races. There should be a planned policy **to help them live in our social conditions**, if they wish, as Aborigines and not as our inferiors.

Letters, B Taylor. Mr Sawtell's desire to keep Aborigines away from white civilisation "as far and as long as possible" reflects a very unreal and, I may say, proprietary, attitude.

The vast majority of Aborigines already live on the fringe of white society and to some extent depend on it. It is a hundred years too late to think of total apartheid.

We have no reason to suppose that Aborigines would prefer it; rather, they are like Tantalus, hungry for what they constantly see and cannot have. Does Mr Sawtell want them driven into some vast human Taronga, there to forget what they have seen – or does he mean they should be left in their present limbo of La Perouse and river banks?

The case of Namatjira's refrigerator notwithstanding, there is plenty of evidence that, given opportunity, the Aboriginal can make a worthy citizen. Let us not deny him the opportunity on Mr Sawtell's recommendation. A little of the Queen Mother's compassion would not be unbecoming in one interested in the welfare of the native.

The statement that "blacks... have no house sense" is of course irrefutable. Any psychologist knows that "house sense" is purely hereditary. Oh, Mr Sawtell!

NEWS AND VIEWS

Letters, C M Scott. Your Staff Correspondent's article on "Women Without Hats" prompts me to mention another noticeable thing which I think may be the result of the "no hat" cult. It is the number of fairly young women one sees in this country with grey or white hair.

Could it be that the sun's strong rays gradually bleach the hair on unprotected heads?

APRIL NEWS ITEMS

The Norwegian ship, *the Skaubryn*, set sail a week ago for Australia. **It carried 1,283 passengers.** In the Indian Ocean, it caught fire, and **all passengers were safely rescued after a period in lifeboats.** The intending migrants were mainly on **assisted passage**, though there were nine Australians.

The Taxation Department issued a ruling that said that a schooling **taxation deduction** was allowable **only if the school insisted that children wear a school uniform.** In 1958, most primary schools and secondary schools had no uniforms, or perhaps had only optional uniforms....

The exceptions were the larger private schools, and more affluent State schools. The ruling came under immediate criticism saying that the new regulations **would benefit the rich to the detriment of most of society.**

Nikita Khrushchev was the newly-chosen Premier of the USSR. He made a few early speeches in which he said Russia was prepared to stop nuclear testing regardless of what the US decided. So there was currently **some hope that his reign would not be as belligerent** as the Russians had been in the in the past....

But the mood in the West changed when he told the satellite States that surrounded Russia that any counter-revolution in these States would be crushed. He also warned the Western nations **"not to stick their pig's snouts in our socialist garden."**

Comment. Hopes of a docile, moderate, Russia were somewhat dampened by this outburst.

In Melbourne, an ex-WWII veteran who had been receiving psychiatric treatment **killed his wife and his four children with an axe**.

The Catholic Church in Australia is in a **non-stop mean and spiteful battle** with the Protestant Churches. Both sides can find good reasons why the other side is bad and not upholding Christian values. They are at the moment at logger-heads over the Opera House Lottery, which the Protestants very much oppose. They also oppose **housie-housie** and many other forms of gambling debauchery....

Catholics have now taken the debate to a new level. The Christian Brothers sect has bought the land-mark Manly Hotel in Sydney. This might be seen as the ultimate sin by Protestants. But it has gone one further step towards the gates of Hell. It is now **proposing to run an Art Union with the hotel as a first prize.**

April 18th. Australia's **first nuclear reactor** was opened at Sydney's Lucas Heights by Bob Menzies.

In Broken Hill, teenage lads who want **a crew haircut must pay one shilling extra**, and bring a note of consent from the parents. This is because of the extra Labor needed for the cutting, and because barbers are often confronted **by angry parents** the next day demanding the barber put the hair back.

Prime Minister Menzies continued a line he had pressed previously. **Automation**, the use of machines to do the jobs of humans, was on the increase. He argued that it in fact gave all people cheaper goods, and was welcome. **The trade unions appeared to think differently.**

ARTIFICIAL INSEMINATION

Insemination was not a topic that was on everyone's lips. It could be discussed in farming circles for animals, but it was, to date, rare to see it raised in connection to women.

Comment. The Letters below give a good picture of where adventurous society stood on this issue, though it is true to say that society in general was not yet prepared to openly discuss it.

Letters, "Frustrated Mother". It is a pity that some leading churchmen cannot find anything better to do than condemn childless women who resort to artificial insemination to satisfy their maternal urge.

Having myself suffered the pangs of a strong, frustrated maternal urge, I know just how these women feel, and after my own experiences with adoptions, foster-mothering State wards and so on, I consider artificial insemination to be the best solution of all, and **only wish that it were legal in Australia**. At present it is only legal if the husband is the donor.

It is a sad position that a woman should be so placed that she must literally beg for any kind of child or go without. How much better if I could have one myself from a healthy donor, knowing that chances of mental, physical or inherited diseases were very remote!

Letters, Douglas Vann. A correspondent recently deplored the illegality of artificial insemination (donor). Whilst insemination of an adult, consenting woman by a man other than her husband, whether by artificial or traditional processes, is not legal, neither is it a criminal offence.

Unless her husband objects, only the Christian ethic remains to restrain a woman from seeking impregnation elsewhere for, if she does not acknowledge spiritual authority, conventional social sanctions can be circumvented, and the material aspect of her problem is simplified to one of search. A more orthodox and innocuous solution to sterility is adoption.

PUBS AND ART UNIONS

The Catholic Christian Brothers' proposal to run an Art Union lottery for the Manly Hotel stirred many passions. Letters poured in from the middle of the month and were still going strong at the end. The best I can do is give a summary, with a few examples.

The Catholics took the view that gambling was not inherently wrong. There was nothing that they could find in the Bible that prohibited it, and there was nothing in modern day ethics or morals that did that either. They admitted that it could be abused, but argued that every activity in life could be abused. Surely it was wrong to stop everyone from gambling because of the few who would abuse it to the detriment of themselves and their family. The solution in this case was to help the sinner, and not prohibit all persons from their quiet flutter and social interaction.

Protestants attacked the scheme on two fronts. **Firstly**, they were fortified with biblical references that they said were opposed to gambling. Most common was that people buying tickets were guilty of the sin of covetousness because they aspired to wealth. If they missed out on this charge, they could be blamed for gluttony and lust for worldly goods.

Secondly, There were the arguments based on the social, the moral, and familial dangers of betting at all. Many tales were told of families suffering from deprivation from parents' gambling losses. On the other hand, there was much criticism of the current gambling craze that had started with the Opera House Lottery, and big sums being won at the racetracks.

Then there were the bitchy Letters that took the perceived opportunity to bash the Catholic Church, often using the Bible as a crutch. Sadly, these were often written by Protestant clergymen. But the Catholics added their fair share of vitriol as well.

Letters, A. M. McNamara. Protestant clergy, in their adamant denunciations of gambling, have sought to deny to the Catholic section of the community an **opportunity of raising funds, by voluntary means**, for the furthering of education of Catholic children, which is undertaken without cost to the State.

Letters, N. Morris. The Roman Catholic Church requires £150,000 for the extension of one of its many teaching organisations in this State. By holding out an alluring £190,000 carrot, **it hopes to tempt the Protestant donkey** to disgorge at least £100,000 of this amount. Should the Protestant donkey be so tempted, then it will be entirely responsible for the outcome, e.g., an ever-increasing Roman Catholic influence on all that affects this life.

Should the Protestant donkey, however, decline to sell tickets for, or buy tickets in, the said carrot, the Roman Catholic community will have to devour it to the point of indigestion. In these circumstances, any moralising on the issue will be a matter affecting only the Roman Catholic Church, and no one else need concern himself with it.

The community in general is invited to put up £347,000, of which £190,000 is for a publican and £157,000 is for Roman Catholic purposes. **Any Protestant who supports such a proposition must be dumb indeed.**

Letters, W Coldell. If some 1,200 dedicated men are prepared to educate each year for the highest of motives 50,000 Australian boys without a penny of personal remuneration, I calculate that at present cost levels they are saving my pocket in taxation each year at least the price of a ticket in the art union. So I say good luck to them, and will someone please tell me where I can get a ticket quickly?

Letters, J S M. In this country we sign charters that guarantee freedom of religion and freedom for parents to give children the education they think best, but in effect we maintain savage economic sanctions against those whose conscience dictates an education with a religious background. Not even a book or pencil will be supplied to a child or a stick of chalk given to a teacher unless they are part of the State system.

Letters, James Duhig (Roman Catholic) Archbishop of Brisbane. A much greater scandal than art unions is **the gambling in land and the profiteering in other matters** which is extensively carried on in Australia at the present time. The excessive profits made by dealers in these properties is to my mind a much worse form of gambling than an art union, yet our Governments and newspapers do not condemn it.

There are other examples of profiteering that I might mention which I hold are a major scandal, much worse than anything in the form of an art union.

Letters, A Robinson. The selfish dog-in-the-manger attitude shown by the Protestant clergy towards their fellow Catholic men leaves little to be admired. Every time the question of Government aid to Catholic schools is mentioned, the bishops and clergy are loud in their denouncement. Now when the Christian Brothers organise a method of raising finance for the welfare of our Australian children, the same voices are raised again.

Letters, (Rev.) Lisle M. Thompson. The argument advanced by your correspondent B McGee is that because a man's money is his own, he has the right to forfeit the title to it if his number remains in the barrel.

This is not Christian teaching. The Bible teaching of the relationship between man and money is that man has no title to anything. Absolute ownership belongs to God. "The silver and gold is mine, saith the Lord. The earth is the Lord's and the fullness thereof, etc."

Man is only a steward of God's wealth, and far from forfeiting his accountability to what he handles, he will **answer for the use of every penny and pound of it in the Day of Judgment**.

Can we blame God for shortage of means for schools, hospitals, houses, roads, and parks while as God's stewards we prefer to spend £430 million a year on drink and gambling, both of which are championed by the Roman Catholic Church?

Letters, Anthony La Spina. Gambling can cause mental distress to the individual, and lead him in desperation to steal and commit other crime. Even a win does not satisfy, for the craving leads him to burn it on the altar of his gambling idol. A home where gambling has even a toehold suffers a loss of grace and dignity.

Is it reasonable that one should ignore present-day observations and the guidance of one's own inner light, and seek instruction from a book written 2,000 years ago, as to whether or not gambling is evil? That is what Dr Rumble requires one to do.

Dr Rumble, a Catholic spokesman, justifies the participation in and encouragement of gambling by the Church by the fact that the Bible nowhere states literally that gambling is evil. Since Dr Rumble insists on scriptural instruction on the matter, it is reasonable to expect him to be consistent and provide scriptural support to many Catholic dogmas which are binding on members under pain of mortal sin. He cannot for example point to anything in the Bible that puts forward the theory of the Trinity.

Letters, H MacDonald. I cannot see that it is our concern how the Christian brothers raise money for their school, nor can I accept the axiom that to have a bet or take a lottery ticket is fundamentally wrong.

Letters, (Mrs) Joan Bond. It seems obvious that the leaders of the Roman Catholic Church, in launching their £190,000 lottery, are taking just another step in their campaign to bring about legislation to introduce State Aid to Church schools in New South Wales, and so cause the Protestant community to be forced to pay, by taxation, part of the upkeep of the Catholic vast educational system.

By drawing public attention to their apparently penniless state, by means of this lottery, they no doubt hope to considerably strengthen their attempt to gain State aid.

Letters, John Axtell. Without regard to the ethics or morality of this orgy of gambling – art union, lotteries, jackpot totes, poker machines and what have you – which is so assiduously sponsored by the State Government, the impact on national and social economy is making itself obvious.

The most distressing aspect of the whole sorry business is **the intensity of acrimonious recriminations** which are incited between opposite schools of thought. It is refreshing to note that some of the clerical protagonists – Catholic and Protestant – have debated the issue in its true perspective, pro and con, without asperity.

Unfortunately, the prevailing tendency on all questions of national interest, economic stability, standard of morality and Christian faith is to resolve themselves into bitter sectarian bigotry or political fanaticism. Nothing is debated on **the firm foundation of logic, sane nationalism, or genuine solicitude** for the welfare of the community as a whole.

Controversy under these conditions inevitably divides well-meaning, friendly people into violently hostile factions, and has an incipiently corroding influence on our way of life and nobler instincts.

Comment. As an observer who has studied the newspapers daily for thirty years in writing these books, I heartily endorse this last Letter. When certain subjects, ranging from religion to fluoridation to teenagers, come up for discussion, all reason goes out the window, and long established ideas, often just plain bigotry, flood the Letters pages of newspapers.

NORTHERN AUSTRALIA

Letters, Michael Sawtell. I am delighted, indeed, that Mr Muggeridge has sensed the vast potential of our north.

Since 1901 I have seen Alice Springs grow from 29 white people to 4,000, The Catherine from a publican and a policeman to 600. In 1908 I lived one year at Humpty Doo, and when I used to see the beautiful flooded black soil river flats, I used to ask: "Can't we do something with this country?" And I was told: "There is one thing that we can do with it, and that is give it back to the blacks," and now they are growing record crops of rice there.

Alice Springs is an enchanted land, that some day will be the capital of the inland, and perhaps of all Australia.

Letters, Michael Sawtell. In his article about our Aboriginal problem, what Mr Muggeridge said about the £2 or £3 a week and keep for the ward Aboriginal can be most misleading.

Those wages and conditions are in agreement with the North Australia Workers' Union. All exempted citizen Aborigines all over Australia are paid full award rates. I go out every year to have a look round and after 57 years' experience and many years a cattle man and drover, I wish to pay a tribute to the squatters – they treat their Aborigines splendidly.

We have a stern social duty to help our Aborigines, but we must fully understand that we cannot detribalise them without demoralising them.

There is a more and spiritual gap between their tribal life and assimilation, which will take many generations to bridge.

I also agree with what has been said about the missionaries. With more zeal than discretion they frown upon the most ancient and **spiritually significant myths of the Aborigines, but want them to accept the myths of the Old Testament.**

The Aborigines think that if the story of the Serpent in the Garden of Eden is true, why is not the story of the "big fellow snake" in their myths true. All this leaves the Aborigines confused.

Silly comment. I would like to encourage any of you whipper-snippers who are looking for a topic for a Masters in History or Sociology to look at the life, opinions, and writings of Michael Sawtell as a possible topic.

HOUSING

About 70,000 new houses were built in Australia last year. Only about 2,000 flats were built. This was because renting laws made it impossible for investors to get decent returns on flats. It was too early for home-units yet.

A BRUSH WITH THE LAW

Two policemen in a patrol car stopped a driver at 4am on the outskirts of Melbourne. The driver had **five sheep in the back of the car**. He was a toy salesman, and said he had **won them hours before in a country pub**. He wagered on the fall of a coin, and lost several woolly toys and a mechanical dog, but had won six sheep. One of these escaped.

The police doubted his story, and questioned him back at the police station, and held the sheep. They enquired of the publican at the country pub, and found **the salesman's story was accurate. He and the sheep were released.**

THE END OF TRAMS

The NSW Government decided that it would cost too much money to sell off Sydney's trams. The high price of moving them was cited, as well as the normal costs in advertising and selling. So, it burned them. Photos of the destruction were carried in the Sydney Daily's, and this got quite a lot of blood boiling.

PHONY WORK BY THE PMG

The Post Master General was responsible for running our mail and telephone services. In fact, it had a monopoly on these, so that **it could get away with murder**. It did this with success for years, and so our phone services were miles behind those of the other Western countries.

By 1958, however, the PMG decided to stir itself by changing the dialing system in Australia. So that now the two-letter prefix followed by four digits would give way to a six-digit number. This was not to be seen as just window-dressing, because it allowed for subsequent changes that would allow for more sophisticated equipment to be installed.

In the meantime, the phone service was bad. In a country town, or a typical suburb, there were typically half a dozen public phones, and only dozens of private numbers. Most of the public phones were vandalised as soon as they were repaired, and apart from that, dealing with operators was always a gamble. Private numbers were there only for the wealthy, or the professionals, and a handful of shops. The concept of ordering goods via the phone was unheard of. The hope of correcting some governmental folly by phone was negligible. Party lines were useful for teenage girls to gabble on, and for frustrating other uses by listening-in, and by not hanging up.

The only reliable component of the phone service were the lines to SP bookies. They never had to complain about the prices and information that they lived by, and the punters could always get a line to place a bet.

It was good to see that **the important societal functions had top priority**.

MAY NEWS ITEMS

As more and more people become fearful about the terrible consequences of an A-bomb war, the slogan *BAN THE BOMB* is appearing painted on buildings and sites all over the nation. Even **a US navy warship in Sydney Harbour** woke up the other morning with the slogan painted on its side.

In Indonesia the rebels, trying to unseat the central government, appear to have failed on the battlefield, but have now turned to **destroying the nation's economy.** Thus they have said that they will use their planes to bomb **any vessels entering or leaving Indonesian ports**, regardless of nationality....

The huge Dutch oil company, **Shell, has stopped production** at its Indonesian oilfields because of the threat, and this will quickly wreck the economy if it persists.

The arguments over gambling continued. At a Council meeting in the small NSW city of Bathurst, a butcher argued that poker machine losses were affecting the birth rate in the city. "Women, who are deprived of the money needed to raise their family, **are refusing to have more children.** It's that, or **give up their beauty products....**"

Protestant Churches round the nation have declared the second week in May to be Decision Week. This is a campaign to discourage all citizens from gambling for the week. The Churches on Sunday **gave sermons against the perceived vice....**

The Air Force Association, a national body, has applied for permission to run an Art Union, again with a prominent Sydney Hotel as first prize. The profit would be used to finance a Chapel and Memorial for the airmen killed and maimed in the two World Wars. Given that there is no religious side to this, **will the resistance be as strong as in the Christian Brothers case?**

Front-page news in the *SMH:* Princess Anne to have her tonsils out. The next day, we were assured that her operation had gone well, and that she had awakened to see flowers from her family. The day after, it was a great comfort to all to find out that she was still doing well, but was a bit lonely because she was screened off from the other children in the ward. **All of this was front-page news, and was taken seriously by many readers.**

The New York Zoo had hoped to get a Red Panda from China to exhibit. It would have been the only one in America. The US State Department has refused it entry because **"it is a resident of Communist China"**, and because its entry would have violated the law against trading with that country.

The NSW Country Party is the third largest political party in the State Parliament. At the next election, the major plank in its platform will be **the banning of poker machines in the State**. It hopes to capture the housewives' vote by so doing...

Comment. As one Bathurst editor put it, the Party "appears to have been listening to a few empty vessels, and not to the voices of the silent majority."

FUN DAYS ON SUNDAYS

The nation's churches were keen to spread the Gospel. One way of doing this was to catch children, fresh from the crib, and educate them in their own versions of Christianity. The Catholic Church had set up a school system across the nation that took young people from the age of five and gave them religious instruction until they left school at the age of seventeen. Brothers and nuns and priests, themselves fully educated, co-ordinated this, and the result was that their youngsters hopefully left school with a working knowledge of the fundamentals of the Christian religion.

Most Protestants school-leavers lacked most of this. Granted there were special schools for a relative few of the relatively rich. For example, the Grammar schools in the cities and some rich country areas provided religion as a subject, and many also held daily church services. But for most non-Catholic children, and most of these were in the State schools, they were restricted to about one hour of religion per week in school, and they could avoid this if they elected to do so.

The Protestant churches and many parents however, sought to rectify this by opening Sunday Schools for an hour or two on Sundays. This happened at most such churches round the nation, and allowed instruction in the major lessons from the Bible. The tutors were almost always willing volunteers, female, and many of these were in their grandmothers or in their teens. Together across the nation, they provided much-needed lessons in the basics behind our ethics, morals, and customs.

Sometimes, though, as in all things, good intentions end up with bad results. Complaints were coming in to the newspapers saying that volunteer scripture teachers at State schools were promising that if children went to the beach on Sundays, then God will drown them. Or that if they failed to go to Church on Sundays, then God would slam the gates of Heaven in their face. In Sunday Schools, it was reported that a few teachers were painting such graphic pictures of the events leading up to the Crucifixion that littlies were having nightmares.

Happily, there were some apologists willing to speak up. The first of these gives a glimpse of the difficulties in the job of the teachers.

Letters, (Mrs) Gwen Wade. Many Christian people have read with regret the comments appearing this week in "Column 8" in connection with religious instruction in schools.

It cannot be denied that teachers of the young must be very careful how they phrase their statements, but the irate parents are probably quoting their children's version of what the teacher said – and children cannot always be relied upon to transmit such statements verbatim.

As such a religious instructor, I would like to point out what a difficult task it has proved this week to convey to infant classes the true meaning of Easter. Their minds have been so filled with "Easter Bunny" by parents and school-teachers, that the benevolent bunny is the only symbol most children have of this great Christian festival.

While never wishing to deny any child a harmless delight, I do think that a great deal less importance could be attached to the Easter egg, and a great deal more to the magnificence and wonder of the death and resurrection our Lord Jesus Christ.

Letters, (Mrs) M Smith. There have been several unflattering references to scripture teachers in State schools in "column 8" this week. May I be permitted to say a word in our defence? There are always exceptions, of course, but generally speaking, scripture teachers are a hard-working band who gladly give their time so that children, a great many of whom have no other religious instruction, may come to know something of the Word of God.

Most of us, I can assure you, would never dream of telling any little child that "God would slam the door of Heaven in his face." I, personally, have a deep affection for all the children I teach, and my chief aim is to bring them to the knowledge that God is a God of love, infinitely tender and compassionate.

Letters, M Love. I find on inquiry of my own children that fanatical fire-and-brimstone statements are frequently introduced into scripture lessons. The effect of this, of course, is harmful, both psychologically and to the child's attitude towards religion. The child is virtually taught to fear God and to regard religion as a bogy.

The nature of a child's mind can be shown by its reaction in one example. Recently my five-year-old daughter, not normally a timid child, crept into my bed too terrified to remain in her own because of the too-vivid picture of the Crucifixion painted by her scripture teacher.

It is all very well to claim that children have not given accurate accounts of what their scripture teachers have said, but the fact remains that because of the method of instruction, a fear has been planted in the child's mind.

The Department of Education exercises no control over scripture teachers. They are not employees of the Department. Scripture teachers for senior classes are usually minsters of religion and with their teaching methods there can be no quarrel.

However, teachers of infant classes are, mainly, lay officials. It is with a small group of these well-meaning but misguided people, many of them elderly spinsters, that the trouble appears to lie.

The Department is content, apparently, to allow ministers of religion to choose scripture teachers for infant classes from among these lay officials, and that is as it should be. But, surely, the time has arrived when the Department might ask ministers to exercise every care in the choice of these teachers.

In the hands of these women is the religious training of many children. Are they to beset children with fears and misgivings about religion or are they to treat it as the wonderful study it is?

Letters, (Mrs) F E Thomason. How can we expect a very young child to understand the mystery of the Crucifixion, when adult minds cannot fully explain all its aspects?

The little girl who was so terrified, after being told all the details, evidently reacted in a different manner from another child who had been told about it. Discussing it with another child, he explained, "It must have been faked, like they fake the things in the films."

Letters, (Mrs) Y Crook. M Love does surprise me that in this modern age of "blood and thunder" films and comics there is even one child left that can be so affected by a story of suffering and death of Christ, as she says her child was.

That the scripture teacher was able to so move the child at least speaks well for her capacity for portrayal – at least

M Love should not complain that the teacher lacked that ability.

If M Love objects to the methods of her child's scripture teacher, and if she is not deliberately trying to bring scripture teachers as a whole into disrepute, the correct thing for M Love to do is to approach the special teacher concerned and explain her feelings on the matter to the teacher concerned, and not to assume that all teachers everywhere are teaching in the same way.

Another volunteer teacher wrote that she was well equipped to teach Scripture in all locations because, as a Methodist, she had done a six-week one-hour-a-week course on how to instruct children. This laid emphasis on avoiding lurid descriptions and concentrating on the love of God.

She ended with "I am sure that no woman trained in this Methodist Centre would be guilty of the unintelligent bigotry described in your columns."

Comment. There were a number of other writers who made the point that while many of the teachers were untrained, many of them were untrainable. They pointed to the fact that some of them were so rabid as to be almost fanatical about religion, and about the suffering of Jesus, and about the superiority of their own denomination of religion. These people, it was said often, were well intentioned, but would never be able to present balanced views. Yet, it was hard to sort these persons out from the volunteers who once presented, and once appointed, were very difficult to control or remove.

Another side to the issue was that most of the Protestant churches, like the Methodists mentioned above, had active training courses running all the time to guide teachers with how-to-teach instruction. They acknowledged that there could be some improvement and expansion of these, and that was what they aspired to.

COMPUTERS ARE COMING

Some of you will remember the days when mail was delivered twice a day, and when Post Offices were open on Saturday. Some will also remember that if you wanted to send a quick written message to someone, you could visit a Post Office and watch while the Post Master tapped the message out using Morse Code. And all of you will remember the early days of phone when there were two phones boxes to serve in a town or suburb of 2,000 people, and one of these was always broken.

So, I suppose everyone will agree that our world is a better place now with the advent of computers and the various ways they now make it possible to communicate. Then, to go one further, they can also be seen as improving our lot by the way they process a huge mass of data, and despite worries over perhaps sinister applications, make possible business applications not dreamed of back in the post-war years.

But such a sanguine approach was not always accepted. Back in the 1950's, workers in the Western world were worried about how the new fad of automation would affect their jobs. Maybe it was true that efficiencies could produce goods more effectively, but what about the livelihood of workers? What jobs would they have?

After all, most people thought they had jobs for life, and that what they didn't know about their own job wasn't worth knowing. No machine could possibly replace them.

Sadly, maybe, machines could do just that. Not only in the manufacturing industry, but also wherever large quantities of information were generated and stored and processed.

In Australia, the insurance industry was thus the first one under threat, as punch-cards, then paper tape, and then discs of various types mechanised the industry. Another early application was for inventory control.

By 1958, the writing was appearing on the wall, and workers were starting to seriously dig their heels in. But, as you might expect, there were plenty of experts round with reassuring messages.

Letters, E S Burley. Regarding this statement [that electronic machines will replace clerical staff in business offices in the near future], the average clerical worker is bound to reflect on how soon he or she will become obsolete Fears will be expressed that the application of computers to data processing will cause serious unemployment problems and create hardship and ill will, and it is these fears that I would attempt to dispel.

In Australia, at the present time, we do not have one commercial electronic computer of any significant size in operation.

Actually electronic systems that will do the routine work of many clerks will be needed to forestall a serious shortage of adequate clerical help. It has been evident for some time that the productivity of industry, and an ever-increasing ratio of clerical to production workers has been required to meet the information needs of business and government. Electronic machines will increase the productivity of our clerical force and partially offset this trend.

There is no doubt that some clerical workers will become redundant, but dislocations even within one company will not be as troublesome as many people now imagine. It takes many years to plan and install an integrated data-processing system completely, and by the time the whole computer program is installed normal wastage will generally have eliminated **any** surplus staff without wholesale retrenchments.

As in the case of other technological advances, new jobs will be created. A new profession of data processing is arising to cope with system analysis and design, programming machine operation, and the constant improvement of machine applications.

Office workers in the future, far from becoming obsolete, will have much more interesting work to do, machines will absorb the dull repetitive routine of data-processing, leaving to the clerks the more varied work of establishing controls, making decisions and interpreting results.

Nodding wisely, a Mr Prentice agreed with the above Letter and added a thought.

Letters, T W Prentice. While there is an inevitability about the introduction of such developments into the office (and for that matter industry generally) it is just as certain that unless modern techniques are used in the office we will face a grave shortage of clerical help in the not-too-distant future.

As pointed out by Mr Burley, the introduction can only be gradual, and I agree that while some Labor may be diverted into other channels we need not fear that the introduction of EDP will cause unemployment.

There was, however, no shortage of different views.

Letters, J G Abbott. Your correspondents Burley and Prentice really live in a land of make-believe if they think that electronic data processing machines will not displace clerical workers. Those honeyed phrases used by Mr Prentice about "Labor being diverted to other channels" and "a certain amount of redundancy" deceive no one. Unemployment is inevitable – only a machine salesman would believe otherwise.

When General Motors set up their latest installation in Detroit they laid off over 2,000 clerks. Did these clerks suddenly become tradesmen or did General Motors just forget them?

FOX HUNTING FOR FUN

Appin is a region about 40 miles from Sydney that is famous for its apples. It is located at the foot of the Great Dividing Range, and has lots of cleared land and rolling hills that swirl with mist in the winter. It also had a problem with foxes that ate lots of the animals and pets associated with farms.

Naturally, it had recently been decided by locals that a fox hunt would make a dent if the fox population. So a date has been set, and the locals are getting hold of red jackets, and practising the shout of *tally ho,* and training their labradors in what blood is.

This all sounds like jolly good fun. But not everyone thinks so.

> **Letters, (Mrs) M Duncan.** It was with shame and disgust that I read in Column 8 of a real foxhunt to take place soon, and cannot understand your paper giving prominence to such deliberate, wanton cruelty to a defenceless animal.
>
> This pack of dressed-up huntsmen no doubt consider themselves a fine sporting body to chase a small, terrified animal for miles until it is either caught or drops from exhaustion and is then torn to pieces by the hounds.

In the opinion of many, however, they are nothing but a pack of **blood-lusting sadists, some of whom I fondly hope, may break their worthless necks on the hunt**.

But the indignation felt by the above correspondent was not shared by this gentleman below from another farmland with a similar topography.

Letters, H A Lindsay. It is with amusement that I read Mrs M Duncan's letter describing her shame and disgust at the fox hunt to take place at Appin.

I have been hunting, trapping and baiting foxes for the past 10 years to try to rid my farm of a blood-lusting pest, which, when one sees what it does to an innocent fowl, makes one as sadistic as the hunters of Appin.

Good luck to the hunters of Appin. I wish them a good day's sport and can assure them that if they run out of foxes in their own district, they will be welcomed with open arms by the residents of Annangrove.

BE CAREFUL WHO YOU MARRY

A NSW **man married his aunt in 1944**. It was dubious that the marriage was legal, and he and his aunt separated. In 1946 **he married another woman**, and they now have six children. He applied to the authorities to find what his marital status was. **He was charged with bigamy.** After some hearings, a judge said his first marriage to his aunt was null and void, and that **he was innocent of bigamy**.

JUNE NEWS ITEMS

A **door-knock appeal** from Victorian anti-cancer groups netted about 300,000 Pounds. The volunteer collectors knocked on the doors of about 500,000 homes in the Melbourne area, and asked for donations. This activity was supported by messages over radio and via TV. The result was a spectacular and unexpected success....

Following this, **door-knock appeals became very popular** for a decade until they wore out their welcome.

The Sydney Turf Club will try a daring experiment. From January next year, for a trial period, **it will ban bookmakers from its mid-week race meetings**. Punters at the track will have only the tote to bet on....

It says that more money through the tote will provide for larger prizes and thus generate more excitement and thus bigger crowds. They cite the situation in America, where on-track bookies are banned....

Comment. I expect the experiment to fail dismally. Oz **punters get half their fun from wresting the best odds they can from bookies**, and to have a single uniform price from the tote will not satisfy them.

A number of rare Chinese stamps have been **forged by someone in Australia,** and sold in London and New York. Police have tried unsucessfully to find the source....

This News Item is a reminder that **stamp-collecting was still a source of much pleasure to hobbyists** and of much income to traders. In later years, **it lost much of its appeal** as the market was flooded by nations who produced more and more stamps expressly to milk the philatelists. But in 1958, the hobby was still gung ho.

The number of **British migrants** had been falling in the last few years. But **we still wanted them**, in preference to all others. So, we have announced rules for assisted British migrant families. Basically it will mean that a British family with any number of children under the age of 19 can migrate to Australia for a total of 20 Pounds. That is, 10 Pounds for each of two parents. They are required to stay for three years.

Radio and TV star Bob Dyer caught a 16-foot white shark while game fishing off the coast of Queensland. It weighed 2,350 pounds, and broke the previous record by 17 pounds.

For cricket followers: **Douglas Jardine died** on June 20, aged 57. Most people would say they have never heard of him, but old-timers will recall **the body-line series of 1932-33**, when Harold Larwood gave **our batsmen some close-ups of a rising cricket ball. Jardine was then Captain of the Poms.**

The Art Union craze goes on and on. A Queensland philanthropist and grazier, Major Rubin, has donated a 3,700 acre grazing property, valued at 75,000 Pounds provided it is used to provide a prize for an Art Union.... This gift will go to Sydney's Saint Vincent's Hospital. Given that this gift can hardly be seen as sinful, and the recipient is absolutely blameless, the Protestant clergy can only criticise it from the gambling point of view. But no more so than Lotteries, so some might approve.

THE HURSEYS IN TASMANIA

A father and son by the name of Hursey were wharf Laborers in Tasmania. They were members of the Communist-controlled Waterside Workers Federation (WWF) and, like all such workers, paid Union dues that were taken out of their fortnightly pay-packet. The WWF knew that they had no hope of gaining seats in any elections, but they also knew that if they could form strong links with the Labor Party, they could gain influence indirectly that way. So they put a levy of 10 shillings on all wharfies to help fund the Labor Party at the next elections.

The Hurseys were members of the newish Democratic Labor Party (DLP) that had been formed with the main objective of thwarting Communist control of Trade Unions. They objected to the levy and refused to pay it.

The union machine went into action and declared the men **black.** This meant that other wharfies would not work in the same gang (of about 10 men) with them. Many workers in the rank and file sent them to Coventry, and they received liberal helpings of verbal abuse. The stevedore bosses said that the determined pair had the right to work, and supported their efforts to return to the waterfront, but hundreds of workers on several occasions jostled them as they went to work, and then refused to work with them. For all of June this situation gradually escalated, until at the end of the month the WWF was threatening a protracted nationwide strike if the pair were still promised work on the waterfront. We will return to this story next month.

Here, however, I will give you a few Letters and comments that were generated during this battle, and discuss some of interesting issues that arose.

Many people observed that if the WWF had any sense, it would have quietly agreed that the twenty shillings it was denied were not worth worrying about. Can the loss to the nation, and the loss on workers' wages from a nationwide strike be justified over a really trivial sum? The WWF argued, as it always did, that it was not the sum that mattered, but the principle. If one person could refuse to pay, then others would do so, and the loss would grow.

The response to this was that everyone in the nation could see how badly the Hursey pair had been treated. Would there be anyone else in their right mind who would suffer this over a payment of ten shillings?

The Letter-writers had their say.

Letters, Errington Harvey. Where does democracy hide out in Hobart? Certainly, not on the wharves.

Under our so-called democracy an individual has a right to support any political party he chooses or, if he so desires, he may evolve one of his own. He is, supposedly, not compelled to support with funds any particular political party as a guarantee that he may attend his occupation. However, these principles that are so dear to all freedom-loving Australians, apparently are not adhered to on the Hobart wharves.

The Hurseys were "jostled, jeered at and threatened with violence," merely because they refused to pay a 10/ levy to the ALP because of this they have again and again been prevented from attending work.

The only conclusion I can draw from all this is that on the Hobart wharves democracy and freedom have been replaced by "mob-rule" and oppression.

What sort of a man is he, who prevents his fellow men from working at their job merely because they will not support one particular political party with funds?

It was galling to many people to see that governments were not taking action.

Letters, D Mackay. Harvey, in his very excellent letter, dealing with the Hursey case in Hobart, ask, "What sort of man is he, who prevents his fellow men from working at their job merely because they will not support one particular political party with funds?"

Might we not ask another question?

What sort of Federal Government have we at Canberra that permits a union, the Waterside Workers' Federation, to have a complete monopoly of certain work on the waterfront throughout Australia, without imposing obligations on this union that the rights of all these workers are safeguarded?

Surely the time has arrived for the Federal Government to take action in this unpleasant affair. **No man is permitted** by an Act of Parliament **to work on the wharves, unless he is a member of the Waterside Workers' Federation**. This grants a complete monopoly to the union, and monopolies also bring with them responsibilities to the general community.

It is up to the Federal Government to safeguard the rights of the individual.

Others urged the Labor Party, the traditional supporter of the under-dog, to act.

Letters, V Ryan. Throughout Australia every true lover of justice and fair play, who happens to be following developments on the Hobart waterfront, must be filled with admiration at the courageous and determined stand being taken by the Hurseys – father and son – in the face of opposition ad persecution where perhaps even their very lives are endangered for a principle in which they, as well as the vast majority of Australians, sincerely believe.

As one who over the years has been a supporter of the Labor Party and has regarded that part as the friend and watch-dog of the underprivileged, the down-trodden, the oppressed and persecuted, I now feel, in view of happenings on the waterfront, that perhaps I have good reason to review my opinion in the face of the political inertia of leaders of that party.

But there were others who had the idea that the majority rules. The WWF, through a show-of-hands had decided to pay the levy. Surely, every one would agree that the majority rules.

Letters, H Tilmouth. Concerning the Hursey matter Errington Harvey appears to be very much in error regarding the vital principles of democracy. A cardinal rule of democracy is the observance of majority rule and the Hurseys have flouted that rule. No one can deny that Labor in politics has been of benefit to the wage-earners. With that fact in view the Hobart watersiders moved to strike a levy to augment A.L.P. funds. It was carried, I understand, by a substantial majority. That should have ended the matter for any real democrat.

I observed during my time of union membership that extreme militants and conservative capitalistic-minded workers were the section ever ready to flout the rule of the majority if it didn't suit them.

In municipal matters people often have to contribute to the cost of something they don't approve, but it would be quite illogical to refuse to pay rates on such grounds. If the Hurseys turn out to be the "worsies" as a result of the dispute they will only have to confront the nearest mirror to gaze on the chief cause of their misfortunes.

This raises a conundrum, and a quite reasonable question. How far can a majority decision go? Can it be used to oppress the minority? The writer below sorts that out.

Letters, S B Page. The acceptance of majority decisions is a principle of democracy only in so far as it is essential to stability of government, or, in some circumstances, to communal well-being. For the first of these requirements we put up with the party system of government which virtually disfranchises 49 per cent of the electorate, and for the second we pay rates for the upkeep of roads which we personally may never use.

Beyond these essential needs (and even within them) the principle has to be applied with extreme caution if we are to maintain the notion that freedom is compatible with democracy. To use it as an excuse for the oppression of minorities is quite contrary to the spirit of democracy. On Mr Tilmouth's line of argument, a Liberal majority Government could force the Labor Party to pay for the next Liberal election campaign (and force the Press to keep the matter secret); or a Protestant country could expel all Roman Catholics or deny them work. The principle could be used – and has been used – to justify wholesale massacre. As members of a "free" and "democratic" nation we consider such suggestions absurd. And yet the persecution of the Hurseys goes on before our eyes.

Why do we tolerate it? It may be that our gratitude to the Labor movement for its contributions to our welfare has reached the stage of idolatry: unionism has become a sacred cow before which the sacrifice of the unfaithful is justified in the name of the cause. But not in the name of democracy.

Comment. Of course, there is no real answer to the question: how much control can the winners have over the losers? In a totalitarian State, the answer is "quite a lot." In a democracy, with all its supposed freedoms, the answer varies. For example, in a Club, the majority rules. Once a decision is made, everyone in theory accepts it. But the WWF is a special sort of club. It had the legal right to grant working privileges, or to deny them, to any workers. Then, under that privilege, have they not the right to deny work to any persons who refuse to accept a voted-on decision?

The answer is not obvious, and that is why the governments and political parties were keeping their heads in the sand at this time.

There the matter rests at the end of the month. The Hurseys have been granted 10 days leave on full pay by the stevedores. This will keep them out of sight and avoid ugly confrontations on the waterfront. They have been served eviction notices from their rented dwelling, and that is undoubtedly connected to their dispute with the WWF. A nationwide indefinite strike by the wharfies is on the cards. So now we wait for what happens next month.

THE DEATH PENALTY

The States had different rules about executing criminal offenders. Most of them by now still had the death penalty on their statute books, but generally commuted the death sentence to life imprisonment. The last man in Australia to be executed was Ronald Ryan in 1967 in Vitoria, and the last woman was Jean Lee in 1951, also in Victoria. But there were dozens of others whose sentences had been who were commuted to life imprisonment.

In NSW, the death penalty was abolished, except for piracy and treason. But a recent case of the murder of a schoolgirl had excited public passions, and the Leader of the Opposition in NSW, **Bob Askin, had stated that he would support its re-introduction for the most heinous crimes.**

He got some support from a few readers.

Letters, C Usher. The timely plea of the Mr R. Askin, for restoration of capital punishment in NSW, at least "for the worst types of murder," should prompt us to consider the object of our criminal code. Humane ideas, however worthy, and long-term objectives such as the reform of the community in general and criminals in particular, are entirely secondary considerations and deflect us from our main purpose.

The object of our criminal code is to give ourselves both as individuals and as a community the maximum protection from crimes, particularly those of violence. If a convicted murderer actually serves a life sentence he may kill a warder, and if he is eventually released he may kill again, as has happened in NSW.

In each case we, as lawmakers, have failed in our duty to the community by failing to give it the maximum protection possible. Opinions may vary as to the value of capital punishment as a deterrent. If it even deters one potential killer, it has saved one life. Also the only guarantee or deterrent against a convicted murderer killing again is his execution.

But there were others, probably the majority, who thought the purpose of prisons was to rehabilitate criminals.

Letters, Joh Aspinwall. I agree with Usher that one of the prime purposes of authority is the protection of the community at large.

If we are to accept the death penalty for murder, then by the same standards a forger requires hand-branding, theft a fine, and assault a flogging. Fortunately as new generations grow, the penalties for crime are being slowly amended to include the social, humane and rehabilitation part of the problem, which your correspondent seeks to ignore. Most of our present penalties allow for the opportunity of making amends and rehabilitation, and these opportunities should not be withdrawn from the criminal when applying punishment. Capital punishment is alone, in that it removes all possibility of a re-education in the convicted person, and one of the few punishments still applying the "eye-for-an-eye" belief in the administration of the law

When the death penalty is abandoned for murder then man's humanity to man will have grown again in the same way as when it was discontinued for theft.

Letters, K W Frost. When an individual, by some shocking crime of violence, displays the brutality of which human nature is capable, it should bring home to society a sense of responsibility, and a determination to reform, rather than a desire to match the example of the offender by cold-bloodedly breaking his neck.

If capital punishment is to be justified by deterring one potential killer, then by the same argument it should be abolished if it executes one innocent victim, and whereas it is a matter for conjecture whether or not potential killers have been deterred, many cases of innocent persons being executed have been proved.

Comment. The discussion then veered away from the rights of wrongs of the penalty, to other matters.

Letters, Constance Howard-Blott. To Mr Askin's plea that much sterner measures be taken against criminals of the worst type, may I suggest an additional reform – **the resumption of policemen on the beat.** This would be a protection for law-abiding citizens and a safeguard for women and children, particularly at night. Had a policeman been on his rounds in the Burwood-Concord vicinity that night, it is possible the murder would not have been committed.

Letters, Onlooker. After a recent trial Mr Justice Ferguson sentenced a man to penal servitude for life and added the words: "You may regard yourself as fortunate that you are a member of a community which will allow you to go on living, instead of having you destroyed like other pests."

I suggest that the Judge should have sentenced the man and left it at that. Let us have the appropriate punishment as prescribed by the law, but not the personal opinions and dogmatic statements of these legal "big shots." There are too many Judges these days making bitter personal attacks against convicted persons.

On the other hand, here is a second opinion.

Letters, Jeremy Horne. "Onlooker" objects to Mr Justice Ferguson telling a murderer in court: "You may regard yourself as fortunate that you are a member of a community which will allow you to go on living, instead of having you destroyed like other pests." "Onlooker," says the Judge should have sentence the man and said no more.

It will be an extremely bad thing if Judges do not exercise their freedom of speech in what they believe to be the public interest, and in the interests of crime prevention. Indeed, failure of Judges to make appropriate comments in cases of grave crimes would create a dangerous impression that such crimes are not regarded as seriously as they should be.

It is safe to say that if someone belonging to "Onlooker" were the victim of an atrocity, "Onlooker" would not object to the Judge speaking out against the criminal responsible.

Comment. Arguments on the death penalty come down to its purpose. Is it to punish, or is it to rehabilitate. The pendulum has now generally swung towards rehab, and most people in their sober moments agree that the death penalty should go.

But having said that, there are moments for all of us, I think, when confronted by reports of vicious crimes, that a mean little person inside us says "Hang the bastard." After a few minutes, that little person shuts up, and we get back to our sober selves. But still, in society in general, those **mean little people** club together in times of revolting news, so that this matter comes up for discussion year after year, and there is always an Askin who sets us all thinking again.

THE BABIES ARE STARTING TO BOOM

Children keep popping up all over the place. Whatever the cause, they have done this for years, and it could be that, welcome or not, they will persist in doing so.

In any case, during the War, many of them made their presence felt, and then after the War, they came out in droves.

By now, in 1958, it seemed that they were everywhere. If you read the Press, it seemed that their sole purpose, as teenagers and children, was to annoy their elders. In particular in trains, they were a scourge. They took up seats, they clogged the corridors, they vomited out the doorways, they dare-devilled out the carriage doors. The newspapers, in their times of slack news, reported with suitable outrage, that a pregnant lady had her seat snatched by "fat schoolgirl with pimples", and that a boy in a boater hat had urinated out of the carriage near Milsons Point. Can you believe it: Milsons Point no less? Obviously, children were out of control.

To keep these urchins under control, entrepreneurs thought up a venture in all the major cities. This was to open up a picture theatre in the centre of the city, and then offer late night movies. The more liberated children and teens flocked to them.

But there were always narks who believed that children should be more restrained.

Letters, Annoyed. In view of the fact that we are to have another midnight picture show on Sunday, I would like to make a protest. The majority of the patrons are teenagers and I think that anything which entices young people to stay out until the early hours of the morning is a step in the wrong direction.

Some, who come from nearby suburbs to attend, cannot catch a train home until 4.30a.m., so is it any wonder that they get into mischief while waiting around for more than an hour and cause the police considerable trouble quelling brawls.

Instead of the newspapers condemning the teenagers for their behavior following these midnight shows, it would be more in order to blame those responsible for having a session at a time when people should be home in bed.

Teenagers, however, were not conspicuous for reading the Letters column of the SMH, so they continued on their merry ways. But one teenage girl did know of the existence of the column, and wrote in defence.

Letters, K Jarvis. I would like to stress the necessity to ceasing criticising teenagers, on the part of adults. (I am a teenager myself.)

Why do you think certain teenagers sometimes perform serious acts? For publicity, of course!

But this part of the community is fortunately comparatively small. Many adults seem to forget (or want to forget!) the Charleston and Jitterbug eras!

Also, adults seem to not notice the many **boisterous and noisy parties which are held by adults** every night of the week. And also the brawls which are started outside hotels every night by older people. You like to forget this part of the community, don't you? Yet nobody forgets those certain teenagers of the community who don't really do as much harm. Another point is, often bodgies and widgies are formed on account of the homes which they come from.

All I am trying to say is, stop gossiping over every piece of "juicy" news about the local teenagers in your neighbourhood, and probably a high percentage of bodgyism will be killed.

Comment. This eminently sensible comment was written by a teen, who would now be aged about 70. I wonder where she is now, and how the years have treated her. If you know her, maybe you can persuade her to tell me what life has brought her.

ECONOMY ON MATCHES

Do you remember pulling out a box of matches from your pocket or purse, lighting the gas or a cigarette or a fire, and throwing out the dead match, and putting the box back in your pocket? Anyone who did any of those vital things always carried a box of matches.

They were thin wooden spikes with a red head, and they came in boxes of 60 that most often had the brand *Federal* printed on its side. They could also be used as the stake in playing poker, and as toothpicks. In all, quite indispensible.

Now, the world was turning upside down. In Australia, firstly, there was the news that, in future, boxes would contain only 50 matches. This brought forth the following Letter. It was published by the *SMH* under the heading of *Passing of a Legend*.

Letters, Stewart Molder. It is surprising to note that Australia's match combine has decided to recognise what has long been evident to the rest of Australia – that the average contents of our matchboxes have been nearer 50 matches than 60 during the last two years.

I hope it will not rely too much on the reluctance of all of us to count our matches and reduce the actual average to 40 matches.

I regret the passing of the familiar legend, "average contents 60." Ever since I have been able to read this simple line has been a sturdy companion.

While wars have erupted, regimes risen and fallen, and nuclear weapons and satellites become our daily newsfare the line "Average Contents 60" has remained with remarkable durability. Now it is to go.

Comment. Even worse was to come. News was filtering through that cigarette lighters were all the rage overseas and that the same mad craze would soon come to Australia. Of course a caring and perceptive Federal Government was starting to protect the local match-making industry by putting big tariffs on the lighters. But still the craze was taking hold here and its arrival in Australia could be expected soon.

Could it be that the end result would be the demise of the wooden matchstick? No one would mind if the little round boxes of **wax matches** disappeared. But **real** matches were an Australian institution, and our good sense and ever-higher tarrifs will hopefully save us from losing one of the nation's figureheads.

FORMALITY IN ADDRESSING PEOPLE

People have got a lot less formal over the years. Remember as a child how many people you spoke to that were addressed with a title. The butcher was Mr Endean, the shop keeper was Mrs Kohler. Everyone had a title, and it really was bad form to skip it.

A few moments ago, I thought that this deference might just have been applicable to the young, and their respect for elders.

But then I remembered that it was not only young people who doffed their lids. Think of your parents talking of other adults. They mainly referred to them as Mr and Mrs. No doctor could be addressed in any other way that by the term Doctor, and then by inference with a capital D. Even the much-hated Prime Minister Menzies, in some circles, was often referred to as Mr Menzies, equally as often as Pig Iron Bob.

JULY NEWS ITEMS

Colin Petersen is back in Australia. Can I hear you asking *Colin Who*? He was the pre-teenage boy who starred in the Australian film *Smiley*. The lad is back in Australia after six months in the UK making a film. He got paid 15,000 pounds for his efforts. The movie was about the adventures of a young lad who wants to buy a bicycle....

He was later the B G's drummer.

Rebels in Cuba were causing some disruption to US interests there. Mind you, their so-called revolutions in that part of the world are happening all the time. Probably the military battles there will fade away and **the leader Fidel Castro will never be heard of again.**

The number of deserted wives in Australia had doubled in the last ten years. Commentators thought this was perhaps the result of hasty marriages in the immediate post-war period. Or maybe it is the start of a long-term trend.

Australia golfer Peter Thompson won the British Open golf championship for the fourth time. He was tired after 72 normal holes, and then two full 18-hole play-offs. So he can be excused for leaving the course and going back to London, but **forgetting the winner's trophy**.

The western world is becoming interested in safety in industry as though mens' lives were important. To promote this, the British Safety Society has commissioned photos of the Queen in full mining safety gear, with a white full length set of overalls, and a miner's helmet and lamp....

The picture is to be distributed to factories and mines throughout Britain and the world. Several miners wrote that a man shovelling coal would not last one minute on the job in overalls. Comment: **For ex-miners only: she did not carry a crib can.**

Events in the Middle East are moving fast. In the middle of the month, the King of Iraq was shot and killed by rebels. Other rebels in Lebanon were attacking the capital, and the US was sending troops and planes in support of the government. Russia was demanding the withdrawal of the troops. The King of Jordan was demanding his so-called right to rule Iraq, and Egypt was moving its troops to the unruly areas....

This news was unsettling for the entire world, and even **insular Australians were watching** with interest and a little apprehension.

A Sydney man has erected a boundary fence between himself and his neighbour on a long block of land. **It is made of vertical telegraph poles stacked side-by-side touching each other, and sawn to a height of 24 feet.** The neighbours have been in dispute for years, and this fence was erected now because the man wants it "for privacy." Council cannot act on the matter because they have **no jurisdiction over side fences**, only front fences.

HUFFING, PUFFING: THE MIDDLE EAST

The nations around the eastern end of the Mediterranean were at each others' throats. The reason was that between them they produced a great deal of the world's oil. This commodity was of increased importance to the western world as diesel replaced coal, and as more cars hit the road, and as synthetics **made from oil** replaced wool and cotton. The West needed oil, and if the supply was interrupted, the West got agitated, and soon everyone in the vast oil complex was talking tough to anyone who might listen.

This was a familiar pattern and it was easy in Australia to shrug and make some comment like "some things never change."

But things **were** gradually changing. The catalyst was the **growth of nationalism** inside all the Middle East nations, and on top of this, there was the **fanatical rivalry between the USA and Russia to enlist them** as their own allies. The obvious result was that over a decade, kings and rulers were deposed, new governments were formed, new despots came to the fore, and friends and foes rattled round in the West wondering who their good mates would be next week.

This was part of a pattern that the world was going through, as nation after nation sought its independence from colonial and dominating powers. Africa, South America, and most of Asia, had armies and insurgents and revolutions and new ideologies seeking to change the old for the new.

And round them, the USA and Russia hovered at all times, interfering and threatening and seducing, ready to intervene directly in some cases, or covertly, at the drop of a helmet. Fortunately for Australia, we had already been seduced, so we missed out on all of the internal conflict that occurred in most other nations.

Be that as it may, and returning to the oil of the Middle East, I enclose two Letters to demonstrate the diversity of argument that the situation there generated. Do not worry too much about the specifics of the Letters. Just **get a glimpse of the many issues** that were bedevilling the directly involved parties.

Letters, Fairgo. Most people hope, with the Rev Alan Walker, there is more Arab nationalism than Communism in the root trouble in the Middle East. But people of wide humane sympathies should not forget that every Arab is not the Arab of the scripture pictures.

Too many people reproach the Western Powers for too much. The fact is they are entitled to look after their oil interests. The whole story of mankind is a matter of looking after the food and other resources that keep peoples alive and working. No matter who gets the profits from oil, **the oil would still be under the sand if it had been left to the Arabs**. This does not mean there are not many injustices in the oil business. Even England has to watch her friend, America, in this matter.

Everyone wishes the ordinary Arab well, but people should not forget that **the story of the selling of slaves going on under Nasser's eyes** would shock even Mr Walker into giving the Western Powers some credit. We should be told a bit more in our papers of this side of the Arab world.

Letters, F Fuller. The Minister of External Affairs, Mr Casey, stated: "Russia would be very glad to turn the Middle East into a neutralist area." This seems to sum up the crisis in a few words. Russia, fearing an attack from the West, supports the formation of a ring of neutral countries around her border. Britain and America, fearing an attack by Russia, try to bolster up pro-Western Governments in those countries bordering Russia. In a situation such as this, both sides should welcome the neutralisation of the whole Middle East. This would eliminate border incidents and provocation which have led to war in the past.

A NIGHT AT THE OPERA

This was once a pleasant experience but now, I am told, it is being spoiled by an insidious new contraption called television.

Letters, Gladys Teece. It is to be hoped that when the Sydney Symphony Orchestra subscription concerts start next month, **no** attempt willl be made to televise those concerts.

Those who have already attended orchestral concerts which have been televised have had their enjoyment of such concerts ruined. The intolerable glare of the lights suspended in the hall, and the resultant heat, have been such as seriously to mar the enjoyment of the audience.

It has been customary in the past to dim the lighting in the hall during the concert; for it is well known that music is best enjoyed when played in a subdued light.

Nothing is more calculated to prevent such enjoyment than to be blinded by glare and to be subjected to intense heat.

THE MENACE OF HIRE PURCHASE

This nation was in the grip of prosperity, and so spending was alive and well. The introduction of TV was stimulating sales, and people everywhere were confident enough to buy a TV on Hire Purchase, as well as cars and vacuum cleaners. But there were worries about that.

The buyers usually had a first and a second mortgage on their house. The interest rate on the HP debt was quoted as eight per cent, but was in reality 16 per cent by proper calculation. So it was likely that many buyers would default on repayments. This was so obviously happening that the Labor Party announced that HP interest rates and disclosure would become part of their Party's platform in the next election. *Buy now, pay later* was under question.

Letters, James D Wall. How long will it be before the Government places a limit on the amount of interest people are forced to pay when buying television receivers on HP?

Recently, I was talking to a father of four children and I was appalled when he told me that the interest on his £200 television set amounted to £88. This means that he was paying interest of well over 40 per cent, which, in my opinion, is nothing short of extortion.

Some retailers are careful not to mention the interest, before **the set is installed for a "free" home trial** with "absolutely no obligation to buy."

Retailers realise that, once the set is installed in a home where there are children, its chances of coming back to the store are very remote. By not telling the customer the interest rate until the set is installed for demonstration, the retailer can be fairly sure of still getting the sale, even if the rate is 40 per cent.

The demand in Australia for television receivers is terrific. All television retailers should give the public a little of the respect that is due to them, by lowering excessive interest rates.

RESPECT FOR THE CENOTAPH

The Cenotaph in Sydney is a memorial to the Australian soldiers who were killed and wounded in the two World Wars. It is a sacred place that is open to visitors all the years, and especially on Anzac Day and similar war-related days. Every city in Australia has its equivalent.

A couple of Letters talked about the respect that the monument deserved.

> **Letters, "Per Adua".** Motorists ignore the four notices situated at the Cenotaph in Martin Place indicating a Dedicated Area. This is a very poor reflection on their intelligence, and shows **gross indifference to the sanctity of the area**.
>
> The same may be said of pedestrians who short-cut across the concrete plinth of the memorial itself in passing from one side of the Place to the other.
>
> As a former RAAF pilot and daily passer-by, it distresses me to see so much disrespect for the monument "To Our Glorious Dead," and I wonder if the city fathers, the police, ex-Service organisations or the custodian of the Cenotaph himself, share my feelings.
>
> If so, perhaps some positive auction will be taken to enforce "notice of notices" without waiting for Anzac Day to pay tributes of respect.

For the second Letter, I should point out that GPS stands for Greater Public Schools, and these private schools educate the sons of the richest and most influential people in Sydney and the country. The hats they refer to are straw boaters.

> **Letters, Ron Levenger.** The Air Force Association has done everything in its power to instill in the minds and hearts of the citizens of Australia, and particularly those of Sydney, the respect which is due to the Cenotaph.

Recently the AFA requested the support of the GPS headmasters in an endeavour to instil suitable respect to the above memorial. The following passages are quoted from a letter sent to them:-

"A number of our State Committee conducted a survey, during which it was noticed that all were contrite and apologised for neglecting to pay respect.

"However, in the majority of cases our members were quite disconcerted to learn from the boys that they **had not been taught to raise their hats**, and, more important still, had not been educated as to the true significance of the Cenotaph."

The Air Force Association came under a lot of fire for this Letter. Firstly, many writers thought he was talking as an elitist, and this did not go down well. Many other writers objected on the grounds of practicality, such as the worker who passes there 20 times a day in the course of his job. Should he doff his lid every time?

But the main objections came from those who thought that deference should be paid only on suitable memorial occasions, and not otherwise. These writers argued that respect was in no way diminished by persons going about their normal day and saving their prayerful reflections for more solemn moments.

Then again, there is this Letter from a completely different mindset.

Letters, R Mellor. In reference to Mr Levenger's letter may I point out that the Cenotaph is merely a pile of stone arranged in an orderly pattern. Any claim to its "true significance" rests only in the mind.

Though Mr Levenger would wish his son to "raise his hat" in its presence, I would not. In fairness, seeing our children attend the same schools, I would suggest that any teaching of this "true significance" be confined to the home.

COACHING COLLEGES

The Letter below is a reminder that education was being seen more and more as way for children to have a better life. Parents across the nation wanted their children to have more security and more upward progression than they themselves had enjoyed. The obvious way was to give them the best that they could, and ensure that they entered adult life with an educational advantage.

So there was a lot of jockeying to get children into the supposedly better schools. Pre-schools were starting to appear, and that meant some kids were one-up on mere kindergarten kids. And after-school coaching, and coaching colleges, were popping up everywhere. These catered mainly for senior High school students who typically were battlers but with a reasonable chance of making the grade.

One parent found this last trend a bit worrying.

Letters, W Ashcroft. Overnight development of coaching colleges on such an unprecedented scale is a disconcerting commentary on our State educational system. The logical assumption from such a unusual growth in this aspect of our society is that there are serious shortcomings and inefficiency in the constitutional form of education.

Parents can ill-afford the high charges demanded for this extra-school tuition, but the psychology used persuades them that their offspring will inevitably fail in this competitive world unless they "keep up with Joneses" and spur young Johnny or Mary to greater efforts by private tuition. And so we find still another form of indirect taxation wished upon us, as a result of our inadequate primary and secondary schools.

If these colleges are to become a permanent integral part of our society, at least let there be strict supervision by the Government as to standards and qualifications in order that the existing exploitation of gullible parents may be stopped.

Personal comment. It seemed at the time that Coaching Colleges were everywhere. Probably you will remember the *Power Coaching College,* with its motto of ***Power is Knowledge****.* In their early years, the first decade or so, they did a competent job, and the actual coaching was done by High School teachers who wanted to make a few quid after school. Myself included.

After that, I suspect that the standard often fell a little, as students at universities and retired teacher retreads also got into the act. The students in particular did not have the knowledge of the syllabus, nor the teaching skills, to do a thorough job, and perhaps the standard fell.

Still, over the years, coaching has helped many students improve their knowledge, and I am happy to acknowledge that they are here to stay.

NEWS AND VIEWS

I would like to end this chapter with a small collection of minor issues that were rattling or amusing society.

The bomb is to blame. The A-bombs were dropped on Japan 12 years ago, and the immediate tragedy of them had faded a bit. So that now, when things went wrong for people, someone said facetiously "Blame it on the bomb." This applied particularly with the weather. As floods and fire and droughts inevitably took their toll, the bombs were blamed as the cause.

Now this clever little Letter quietly mocked this approach.

Letters, G Wachman. Why has no one yet blamed the atom bomb for the prolonged spell of fine weather?

Actions against chickens. Letters, Barrister. Surely the Commissioner for Police, Mr C J Delaney, did not go far enough when he said that if anyone died because of a game of "chicken", the culprit would be liable to a manslaughter charge.

Actually the correct charge would be murder, which is defined by Section 18 of the Crimes Act to include acts done "with reckless indifference to human life," and this is clearly the case with the game of "chicken."

SP betting in hospitals. Letters, Nora Bourke. If SP betting could be made legal to finance the Opera House, why could it not be made legal to finance the hospitals? Any person who has spent time in any of our hospitals knows **how much money goes out for SP bets**. Every person who comes into the wards is commissioned to take out money for bets.

Would it not be better for a stand **to operate in the hospital grounds** (for the benefit of the hospital) than to allow the money to enrich outsiders, who acquire wealth without paying taxes?

Sanitary workers and clergy. Letters, (Ald) A Heynes.
In reporting the General Assembly of the Presbyterian Church you quote a speaker, Mr Stanley Smith as saying: "At present **sanitary carters are paid more than our ministers**." This is ridiculous.

The inference is that these men are **either of poor intellect or in a low stratum of industry, or both**. I consider the statement in very bad taste, especially when it comes from an elder of the Church. Surely if Mr Smith wanted to draw a comparison to show the inadequate pay of the ministers he could have done it in a better manner, for instance, by a comparison with the teaching profession.

The facts are that the sanitary carters are doing a job of work which, to say the least, is most distasteful. It is enough that they are the butt of many jokes, which I am sure they take in good part, but when a statement is made in public such as that by Mr Smith I consider a reply is called for by any serious-minded citizen.

The early space race. The first attempt to send **an unmanned rocket to swing round the moon failed** when it blew up after 77 seconds, the US Army announced.

Money does not grow on trees. Unemployment was on the increase in Australia, though still low by international standards. There was agitation, in all States, for **a four-and-a-half-day working week** that would create more jobs. **This sounded great to workers.**

But they were starting to realise that it would come with **a 10 per cent drop in pay. When that penny dropped, it was not quite so popular.**

AUGUST NEWS ITEMS

The Canberra-Monaro Express was travelling near Goulburn yesterday when the driver's window was shattered by the flapping door of a passing goods-train. The driver was knocked semi-conscious and his eyes filled with tiny shafts of glass and he was blinded. **The dead-man's brake came into action** and the train came to a stop without the passengers knowing of any mishap. This was a new device, and **passed its first real-time test.**

Changes will soon be made to all telephone numbers in the nation. **The two-letter prefix will be dropped for digits.** For example, XA1472 will become 911472. Numbers will still be restricted to six characters.

The Treasurer, Sir Arthur Fadden stopped a lady in the halls of Canberra and trotted out the familiar line "don't I know you?" But **it turned out that he did**, and before she could reply he said "you are Margaret Frazer." And she was. It turned out that **she had nursed him for four months in 1925 in Townsville** "when you almost died of typhoid." **Some memory.**

The NSW Premier, Joe Cahill, said tonight that **toll roads would soon be introduced into the nation**. Governments did not have the finance to pay for all the roads needed, and a toll would be placed on certain new roads as they were built.

Have you paid **your licence fees for your radios and TV?** I remind you that they were payable every year. To make it easier for poor people to pay, cards were issued by the Post Offices, and you could attach stamps to them slowly as the year passed. Then at the right time, you could offer the stamped cards as payment.

Bread carters are up in arms. The developing **chain stores are offering bread at very cheap prices**, and customers are flocking to them. Less bread is being home delivered, and that the carters are losing jobs....

Various price-fixing authorities are being called in to do something, but the chain stores say, correctly, that they can sell the bread cheaper because they do not have the cost of delivery. So they cannot be accused of unfair competition. **Comment. It seems to me that the writing is on the wall for bread carters.**

Figures released today show that **attendances at cinema had been severely cut** because of the advent of TV. Dozens of theatres had closed, and many had viewings only at weekend sessions. A Hoyts spokesman said the industry was "on its knees, struggling for survival."

A coal miner in a Scottish pit **lit a match to light a smoke**. An explosion followed and nine men were killed and eleven badly burned.

NSW racing authorities have said that **the proposed ban on bookmakers at tracks will be abandoned**. A survey had found that racetracks in the US were "dull and colourless", while Australian courses were currently full of "glamour and charm".

THE EMPIRE GAMES

Every four years, like the Olympics, the athletes from a hundred countries gathered together and competed in the Empire Games. The standard was not as high as at the Olympics, but it was pretty good, and the starters won all the acclaim they deserved.

This year, in 1958, two years after the Olympics, it was noticeable that **the spirit of sportsmanship** and friendly competition **still predominated**, and the Empire Games were unsullied by the new win-at-all-costs attitude that had come so noticeably into the Olympics two years ago. There, the Cold War had appeared for the first time, and the major nations turned away from glorifying their athletes and instead counted ad nausium the number of medals that the nations won. What had previously been an incidental now became an obsession, and success was measured in terms of the tonnage of bullion netted.

Back to the recent Empire Games. This spirit of jingoism had not yet entered the relatively harmonious world of the British Empire, so most coaches and competitors were civil to each other, and when pressed, gave radio and television interviews consistent with being a mortal. But there were exceptions.

One of these was the Australian team manager. This gentleman made several speeches in which he took great pride in telling the world how we were a superior team, and how many medals we would walk away with. There was no modesty, no if and buts, no possibility of failure. We were a great team, and greatness was our rightful reward.

Sadly, he gained a lot of Press, right round the Empire and beyond.

Letters, Nigel Lewis. Let's take a look at our sporting ambassadors, **and ourselves**. Among the tennis representatives we have, over the years, become used to their scowling at bad decisions, belting balls about the court at a bad shot of their own making and general precociousness and bad manners.

The public display last Saturday during what should be a friendly international competition, leaves a very disgusting taste in a lot of people's mouths – both here and overseas.

And our Press reporting on the last Olympics, and now the Empire Games, is almost **always full of boastful sensationalism or excuses in defeat**. All of which gets nice publicity overseas.

Maybe it's about time we all had a good look at ourselves. Perhaps our sporting coaches could instil a little real "sportsmanship" into their charges. Perhaps our sporting writers could pay a little attention to the all too prevalent remarks of disparagement about them.

Perhaps the "Herald" could look at the whole question of sporting reporting and confine sensationalism to horse and dog racing, where international critics don't intrude their nosey presences.

Perhaps we all could make an honest endeavor to overcome a very Australian characteristic, well recognised overseas – to praise ourselves continuously and as loudly as possible, and actually to skite about our ability to do just that.

Letters, "Sportsman". When Australia sends a sporting team overseas again, would it be possible to ban all team managers and coaches from making the trip? Failing that, could they receive lectures, before departure, on such subjects as tact, public relations, and modesty? Their boastful predictions have done great mischief to this country. Could not they **study their charges** and learn something from **their** attitude? Our athletes have shown themselves to be reticent about their prospects, modest in victory, and sportsmanlike in defeat. What a pity if their hard-earned victories should be spoiled by the sickening blurb from our officials.

Letters, (Miss) Margaret Duckworth. As an Australian temporarily in Britain, I was amazed and disgusted to hear the television interview of the manager of the Australian team. His words and attitude were arrogant in the extreme, without a trace of any humility which surely befits a person in his position. To millions of viewers he outlined, not Australia's hopes of success in various fields, but Australia's intention of scooping the pool and having come a very great distance with just that idea.

As a visitor to this country, as the spokesman for our competitors and as an ambassador for Australia, his broadcast must have created a very poor impression. I wonder if many other Australians feel as I do, or if they think our prominence in world sport pardons an approach which disregards the underlying principles of good sportsmanship? Does this manager's attitude set the tone for our team or give a true representation of our athletes?

Letters, R Ruhfus, Toronto Canada. Having taken up temporary residence in one of our sister dominions, it has been disquieting to read the account of Australia's role in the current Empire Games as reported by the Canadian Press. Such references as the "dedicated Aussies" "pledging themselves to a first place finish" and "boasting they will win 11 out of the 19 gold medals for swimming" are not meant to be complimentary.

The Australian manager's **refusal to allow his sprinters to attend the opening ceremonies**, and his terse comment that it did not interest him if this action offended anyone, did not come out well in print, either.

The result is that the Commonwealth has the picture of our Empire Games representative as a cocky braggart grabbing up medals in a cold-blooded, business-like manner devoid of the spirit of such an occasion.

The fault seems to lie with the Australian manager and his officials who appear sadly lacking in the department of good public relations. This brings me to the point that perhaps it would be best to pick men for these positions who are skilled in the art of tact and diplomacy, rather than have them measure up to the popular conception of an American fight manager.

Letters, A Arnot. The idea, that Team managers and coaches of future Games teams should receive a few lectures on elementary behavior before going overseas, is a good one.

The Commonwealth Government should make it conditional to granting a subsidy that something of this nature should be done, as the whole idea of a subsidy is that the team should contribute to better understanding and more friendly relations between nations.

By all accounts, the blatant boasting of officials has had exactly the opposite result.

ABORIGINES IN A HELL-HOLE

As I write these books, I am conscious that Aborigines are getting more and different attention from 10 years earlier or even five years ago. The number of Letters being published is increasing every year, and the attitude toward the Aborigines is getting more sympathetic. A few years back, most Letters were stuck in a condemnatory cycle, with heavy emphasis on laziness and drunkenness and resistant attitudes to white man's dwellings

Over the last few years, things are on the improve. More Letters are acknowledging some reasons why they are different, and point out the rotten deal they are getting, and speculate on what might be done to change their lot.

That is not to say that Aborigines have moved into the white man's light. Far from it, as the next Letter will show. It is simply to say that more people are becoming conscious of the injustices and indignities the Aborigines are suffering, and that more and more people are realising that something must be done.

No one had much of an idea of what that something could be, but this sympathy grew as the years progressed, and 10 years later, when the various Governments moved to introduce more enlightened laws, most people by then welcomed them.

But let me go back to 1958. This Letter painted a grim picture.

Letters, Veronica M Williams. The attention of the Government should be drawn to the shocking circumstances of the Aboriginal population at Coff's Harbour.

Until about four years ago these Aborigines (**about 80 in number**) were contented and living in various parts of the town and district and all in useful employment. Then the Aboriginal Welfare Board, in conjunction with the local Shire Council, decided that they should **be rounded up and segregated**. This has been disastrous to the Aborigines.

About one mile north of the town is a huge below sea-level swamp, declared by the Shire Health Inspector to be an unhealthy area and unfit for human habitation. On the edge of this swamp was discovered a narrow sliver of partially dry land and on this, violating health and building regulations, was squeezed a row of disgusting huts, not even fenced. Then the Aborigines were herded in.

The whole locality is lonely and forbidding, being heavily timbered and with an undergrowth of tall swamp grass. Adjacent to the huts is a wilderness of tree stumps and fallen logs, rubbish, broken bottles, mixed with long grass, mud and water, all interlaced with a vigorous growth of lantana and Crofton's weed. The front doors are only a few feet from the Pacific Highway; the back doors overhang this festering swamp, in which skulk the sly-grogger and prostitute-monger.

These people have gone downhill. Drunkenness and depravity are in full cry. Young girls know no other activity but prostitution; boys do nothing but wander the highway breaking bottles and smashing traffic signs. Disease is rampant, many having TB or VD, and due to untrained personal habits, all are infected by the dreaded hook worm. They spend most of their time in and around the village and camp in jungle along the banks of a sluggish creek that flows through the town. Here sanitation is nil, everything goes in the water; the town swimming pool is in this putrid stream.

These Aborigines should be set free and that vile settlement demolished. To a backward community the situation is apparently nothing, but to a civilised outlook it is disgusting.

This was backed up by the following.

Letters, G Hunt, Captain's Flat. It was indeed lovely to read that Coff's Harbour gave the "best" land available to my old friends the Aborigines, but I'll bet you a "quid" to a quondong that if some parliamentary "pooh-bah" had wanted to stable a horse he would have obtained a more salubrious location. Has Coff's Harbour Council forgotten that we have "pinched" about three million square miles off the "Coon"?

At the same time that this situation was being discussed, two Aboriginal families were stopped from occupying houses in good streets by pressure from white would-be neighbours. The families were good honest citizens without any blemish, and the sole reason for forcing them not to come was that they were black. This was the very same sentiment that was disturbing Americans in the South of the US at Little Rock.

One local white inhabitant, expressed her views in a Letter.

Letter, Mavis Olson. I know that the existing inhabitants of our street in Nambucca are catching much criticism in the white suburbs of Sydney and Brisbane. I want to tell you how we feel.

We have been here for years, and have built a beautiful street with nice houses and gardens and footpath-gardens. We all know each other and socialise together, and our children run together in harmony. We know that if a **white** family came to live among us, then it would take them a long time to fit in.

A **black** family would take longer, no matter how worthy they were. They could be the greatest family in the world, but to us, they would be outsiders. They would be people who would take a long time to learn our ways and what we think.

We think thus that a black family would see themselves as outcasts for years. **It would not be fair to them to put them in that situation.** So we hope to nip this problem for them in the bud, and advise them to find a street where there are already Aborigines living there. There are plenty such streets in Nambucca.

Lots of writers did not buy such paternalism.

Letters, (Mrs) Nell Salisbury. I can't understand why the Government allows this sort of thing to happen. After all, we aren't allowed to choose our neighbours. Everyone is entitled to a decent home of his own. I have a good block of land just off the main Western Highway at Emu Plains, and if this Aboriginal family can get help or finance to build a little home, **I will give them the block of land**. It is about 50ft x 145ft, the rates are paid up, and they are very welcome to it. It is one little bit of their own land I will hand back to them.

Letters, H Owen Chapman. I am stirred by Mrs Salisbury's most generous offer of land at Emu Plains. She could not have chosen a happier prospective location for them. I know there is no place in Australia where our half-castes would be more welcome than in the Penrith district. During the last war a few dozen half-caste children of all ages were brought down from Darwin as a wartime security measure to be cared for at Mulgoa by an ex-sergeant, Jim Potter, and his wife. They attended the Primary school and the Penrith High School; and, as they grew up, they were employed locally at the current rates of wages.

Their unexpectedly fine scholastic performance, their prowess at sports, their friendly reception and good standing among their white schoolmates, and their unvarying good behaviour and high moral standards, were such that they completely won the hearts of the citizens of Penrith, who became very proud of them.

When in 1948 those in charge of them decided to move the whole community to Alice Springs, the Penrith Chamber of Commerce forwarded an indignant, but unfortunately fruitless, protest against thus spoiling the excellent prospects of assimilation that were then opening up before them at Penrith.

I should like to make a contribution towards the expenses of this family if a subscription list were opened. After all, we are Australians and not South Africans.

But now we should return to the Hell-holes where we started. The various authorities had taken ten days to compile many facts, and replied.

Letters, Adele Patterson, Coff's Harbour Aborigines' Welfare Committee. The Committee resents the unjustifiable criticism of the Aboriginal people living at Coff's Harbour settlement. There appears to be no foundation at all for the accusations made by your correspondent.

The shortcoming of the cottages have long been realised and have been the subject of **correspondence and discussion** between this Committee and the Aborigines' Welfare Board and the Minister. The Minister then assured this Committee that at least **doors would be fitted to the bathrooms**. Fencing off the cottages would enable the tenants to do more with their grounds, and the Committee has been informed that quotations are now being sought to do this work.

All the evidence is against Miss Williams' statement that disease is rampant. The Department of Public Health regularly checks on Aborigines; while in 1953 there was a 90 per cent infection of round or hook worm, there is now less than six per cent **on the Far North Coast.** There is no TB in the area, there being only two known cases in the Far North Coast area, neither being at Coff's Harbour. Mantoux tests were carried out in this area and followed by X-ray examinations. All coloured people in this area were checked and no adverse reports were received.

The Coff's Harbour Shire health inspector reported that he found no evidence of insanitary habits and that the worst of the cottages was satisfactory.

No evidence of V.D. has been found, and neither the secretary nor the matron of the district hospital had any recollection of a local Aboriginal having been treated.

The statement that the Aborigines previously enjoyed the beneficial influence of associating with the white community is as absurd as the statement that they were forcibly herded into the settlement, and as the references to a "festering swamp" and a "putrid stream." The claim that they have lost employment is also refuted by the facts. **Six** of the tenants have been in regular employment since going there, another has been out of work only because of illness, and the other has been in casual employment.

The greatest sufferers as a result of Miss Williams' letter could well be the coloured children who attend schools in the district. Some at least of the white children will hear about and accept the statements made, shun them and possibly taunt them with the accusations made against them.

Personal Comment. I am not really convinced by this carefully-worded Letter. The fact that doors will be placed on bathrooms does not satisfy me that standards are all that high. And there are statistics that have obviously been juggled to give a good impression.

In any case, you can make up your own mind, and all I can say is that it is a marked step forward that such matters are being **argued in public**, whereas before, everything was kept hush-hush.

BREAD DELIVERIES

By the end of the month, the bread deliverers chose the NSW provincial city of Newcastle to make a stand against the inroads that the local supermarkets were making into their businesses.

As I mentioned in *July News Items*, the bread carters wanted the shops to charge a high price for bread so that the carters could get the same high price for delivering. But the shops in Newcastle announced that each loaf would be **four pence less than the delivered article**, so housewives in their thousands were wending their way to the shops. The carters really had no leg to stand on.

So, like all good workers' groups in the nation at the time, they threatened to strike. This was silly, because it just drove more housewives to the shops. Then a general impasse arrived, and the matter settled down to a war in the papers. This was mainly dreadfully boring discussion of costs of flour, and manufacture, and delivery, and packaging, and reached the inevitable conclusion that anyone can make up any figures to support his case.

But there were a few Letters that were a bit cleverer than that.

Letters, G V Wade. The State Secretary of the Bread Carters' Union, is reported to be about to embark on a campaign against the reduction of 4½d a loaf in the Newcastle district.

As the manufacturer in question can apparently guarantee the quality of his bread, it is a little difficult to see why Mr England is complaining about such a reduction which must benefit the general public, and it is most bewildering to feel that a trade union has, presumably, such high capitalistic tendencies as to desire a commodity to be sold at far more than its market value.

I feel sure that most of the inhabitants of Newcastle couldn't care less about the carters or their union, and as far as Mr England's threatened campaign to stabilise the high cost of bread is concerned, I wish him loads of luck – all bad!

Some bread makers were not without guile, and one of them prepared this seductive Letter.

Letters, F Nesbitt, Secretary, Northumberland Master Bakers' Association. Economies offered by any grand-scale conversion to depot or self-serve bread distribution will be really nebulous and only a mirage. In the background of today's basic wage formula any economies which consumers gain out of the lower price will be very temporary advantages. Bread being a "C Series Index" commodity, the price reduction will reflect itself in the next quarterly wage declaration as **a lower wage**.

On the basis of six loaves per household per week the effect could be a wage reduction of 2/3 a week.

This is a matter of some significance to all trade union leaders and has recently been demonstrated with potatoes. The practical result would be the consumer carrying his own bread and paying for the privilege.

Even your Special Correspondent admits that goods supplied through supermarkets are rarely cheaper and are in most cases dearer.

Before recklessly demolishing the existing delivery structure, care needs to be taken that something less satisfactory, and perhaps more costly, does not arise in its place. Wet and bad weather have been entirely ignored in the chain store scheme and the invalid housewife or pregnant mother does not exist. The new order contemplates the housewife as a strong and willing pack-horse who will not notice the bulk or weight of a few more pounds of bread on top of the burden she already carries.

The public needs to watch that they are not being gulled by a sales stunt which is using bread as a bait to entice the unwary into the self-serve store every day.

Mr Nesbitt did not seduce everyone.

Letters, Alice Murphy. My memory goes back to the hot summer of 1951 when, as a pregnant mother living in West Lindfield, I asked the baker at Lindfield shopping centre if I could have my bread delivered. Shocked to the core, he pointed out firmly that his breadcarter had decided his round should end about 400 yards from my home, and that he could not ask him to go beyond that boundary.

The result was that my three-year-old son and I walked a mile each way to the shopping centre about three times a week and collected our bread from a delicatessen which made no deliveries.

Letters, Housewife. Why are master bakers **handing over their deliveries to bread vendors**, and incidentally avoiding direct contact with the housewife and thereby also her protests about inferior manufacture, unhygienic handling, and in fact too many instances of irregular delivery, all this plus incivility?

What a relief it must be to obtain not only much cheaper bread, clearly wrapped and guaranteed quality to the residents of Newcastle. Here in Sydney we have to tolerate delivery of bread, often after having been dropped in the street, unwrapped, and handled by cigarette smokers' hands who have also mauled dust-covered horse reins and harness generally. I might add that the horse itself is far from an advertisement to the master bakers, covered in sweat or rain-soaked and dejected.

Mr Nesbitt's letter to the Press cuts no ice where a long-suffering housewife and her daily supply of the all-important loaf of bread are concerned.

Three hearty cheers for Newcastle chain stores.

Most writers to the *SMH* were of the opinion that the bread carters were not wanted any more, and that their annoying ways over many years meant that they would get the fate they deserved. At a glance, I would say that there were **more tears spent for the doomed carters' horses** than there were for the carters themselves.

Home deliveries of all sorts of goods were all doomed at the time. It is interesting to note, though, how some of the industry has made a comeback in 2016. From groceries, including bread and milk, to pizzas and full meals, home delivery is as close as your mobile.

Comment. This is a sour point with me. Our postal service has not made a comeback. The prices keep rising, and it is getting harder and harder to have mail delivered to the home in a timely manner. Remember Saturday deliveries. And afternoon deliveries.

SEPTEMBER NEWS ITEMS

Workers employed by the NSW State Government will receive **three weeks leave per annum**. This compares with the current two weeks. This is expected to flow through to other workers in NSW....

A few other States already have this provision as do all employees of the Federal Government.

The Catholic Bishops issued a Pastoral Statement to be read in all Catholic Churches next Sunday. It included that a car driver would **be guilty of a mortal sin if he deliberately drove through a red light**, even though no one was injured. It would also be **a mortal sin to play chicken on the roads....**

"The morality in driving the car is the same as the morality for a man carrying a loaded gun." The Statement went on to say that a person can drive a little faster than the speed limit if he is a good driver. **Interesting logic.**

The Australian economy is being boosted by a number of American firms establishing chemical and tyre companies here. There are complaints that this will mean that **dividends will be paid to US investors and not be kept in Australia....**

But sanity generally prevails, and the influx of capital is welcomed along with the creation of jobs. The common slogan of *"Yankee go home"* does not apply to their capital.

How things can change. During the War and for almost 10 years later, **the miners of the NSW Northern coalfields** were always abused by all and sundry for striking. They rightly wanted better pay and conditions, and wrongly thought that striking, about one day in three, was the way to get them....

Automation of underground mining is in full swing and **miners are being sacked**. The glory days of the pits is over. 600 more miners will go in September and 310 of them will be from a pit called Abermain No 2....

This was my father's pit and he worked all his life there till he was retired, fully dusted. Six other family members worked their lives there. None of these surviving regretted its closure. None of them has fond memories of the place....

Nor do I. Nor did my mother. No child should go to school every day, and no Mum should be in the kitchen, **hoping and praying that the father will not come home dead.**

The British Empire had not long finished playing its Games...

An Australian Rugby Union player was very excited because his **Australian team had just beaten the New Zealand team**. This was a rare feat....

In **a radio interview** straight after the match, he proclaimed enthusiastically that "**we beat the b......s**". The microphone was ripped from his grasp, and several of his team members were upset "because their wives might have been listening." The player himself was also worried by the thought that **his fiancée would have heard him.** He expects that he will banned from interviews after future matches.

POLICE IN THE SPOTLIGHT

A Mrs Melville, a Member of the Upper House in NSW, says that she had a list of a hundred claims of bad conduct by the police. She refused to give details, and the Premier at the moment was refusing to launch an enquiry. It was obvious, though, that the claims did not relate to major crimes, but rather the day-to-day conduct of officers in minor matters.

But let me digress for a few moments. Everyone knew that in 1958 the police were quietly breaking the law all the time. **For example**, SP bookies were in every pub in the nation every race day. They were standing brazenly at the bar, or out the back near the dunny. Any policeman could have walked in at any time, and made an arrest. But this did not happen, because they instead took bribes to turn a blind eye.

Another example. When drivers were involved in a crash. The police often called a tow-truck operator who cleared up the mess. But most times when the operator was leaving, they slung the police a small bribe.

In most of Australia, this was the accepted order of things. People might go tut-tut, but no one was surprised by Mrs Melville outrage, and no one thought there was much to it. However, the Premier and the Police Commissioner could hardly take that attitude, so the political rumblings were substantial, and commentary on them made them both sweat.

There were many issues involved. I give you a small sample.

Letters, LEGALITY. Many practitioners feel that it is extremely difficult to overcome the **unconscious bias towards the Police Force that exists among magistrates** when members of the force give evidence in cases before them. Many magistrates know the police witnesses personally and there is not the element of impartiality which exists in Quarter Sessions where the Judge is appointed from the ranks of practicing barristers. I claim to be a law-abiding citizen of over 60 years standing and have always had a very high regard for the great majority of the Police Force – but I consider Mrs Melville has aired a subject that badly requires airing.

Letters, Harold Simpson. Some time ago I had occasion to go into the witness-box for the first time in my life in connection with a traffic offence. I left that court disillusioned and with doubts that justice was always done in at least minor offences. I gained the impression that when evidence is being given **by two policemen to a magistrate, other witnesses**, no matter what their standing, **are given very little credence**. Without doubt it is believed throughout the country that when evidence is to be given by two policemen before a magistrate in traffic offences, in most cases it is impossible to avoid a conviction and the simplest thing is to plead guilty.

In these days, when it is essential that drunken and dangerous drivers be punished with the greatest severity, it is also essential that we have complete faith that the innocent person is not convicted. I for one have had my confidence shaken in this respect and if, as I think is quite apparent, there are a great many others of the same opinion, then there is a grave danger that our complete faith in British justice will be undermined.

Letters, A Conway. There is one aspect of police behaviour overlooked in the present controversy – their sensitivity to financial, political and social standing of persons with whom they come in contact. A case, still fresh in the public mind, of a year or so ago concerns a constable who arrested a man on a driving charge.

This policeman abused the driver in insulting terms only to find, with a shock, that he had one of Sydney's most distinguished surgeons on his hands. In his abject apology **the constable excused his conduct on the ground of his ignorance of the citizen's identity**. The surgeon replied, with emphasis, that "who he was" should have no influence whatever upon the policeman's behaviour to a person apprehended.

Letters, Claude Barnett. Surely the Deputy Leader of the Opposition is correct in saying that Mrs Melville has indicted the government as much as certain police officers. If only half of what she alleges is correct, it can only mean continuously lax administration over a long period.

Letters, E W Baxter. Mr Cahill and his Ministers have become complacent from many years in office. They are so engrossed in holding power in their hands that they have forgotten the principles of justice, freedom and the sanctity of individual rights from which their party once drew its inspiration and its strength.

There was a time when the mere suggestion, let alone clear evidence, that ordinary decent citizens had been cruelly treated, browbeaten, intimidated or abused by the police would have set the Labor Party aflame and brought instant action from its leader. It is not so today. Mr Cahill and his henchmen have been corrupted by power and by the privileges of office.

Let them beware. There must still be within the Labor Party many who have not forgotten their principles and who know that "the price of freedom is eternal vigilance." Also there are many such as myself who have supported the Labor Party in the past but whose respect for civil rights and the decencies of life goes deeper than party loyalty.

I hold no brief for newspapers but in this State at this time if I was the victim of injustice or brutality and I had to choose between going to the head of the Government or the newspapers for help I have no doubt to which I would go.

Letters, Mrs B J Pinkerton. I am, like your correspondent Harold Simpson, a law-abiding citizen who had every faith that justice could always be obtained by any citizen. My illusions were also shattered through being a witness for a person charged with a traffic offence.

I was dumbfounded that the two policemen concerned did not tell the truth and even more amazed when (outside the court) the solicitor advised the person charged not to appeal against the very heavy fine as it "was useless to argue with the police." I reprimanded the solicitor for his cynical attitude and asked him why the magistrate had made the decision he did. His reply was that "the magistrate will always believe the police story against a witness."

I was so incensed that this seemed to be the case that I myself sought legal advice a few days later on what I could do to have this matter brought to the notice of the Minister of Justice. I obtained a copy of the Court depositions which when read seemed a travesty of the true events.

After much letter writing, we have reached nothing but brick walls, the answer being that investigations have been made and nothing can be done (the investigations were conducted by the police against the police), and I understand how Harold Simpson and others have had their faith in British justice sadly undermined – mine is now non-existent!

Letters, Queensland Barrister. Police are hated and feared – and the sooner we have the courage to face that fact the sooner will things be altered. However, I expect Mrs G Melville, MLC, to get exactly nowhere. The power of the police is too strong. Your paper is to be congratulated on its intelligent view presented through its editorials and letters from the public.

Letters, George R Johnson. There seems to be a considerable difference in the English and Australian (or at least NSW) police ideas as to **when a person should be arrested for drunkenness**.

In England, if a person "under the influence" is behaving himself and not causing a nuisance to himself or other people, he is advised to go home and sleep it off. The only time arrests were made was when the person was helpless (when it was for his own protection) or disorderly.

During the first week of my arrival here I saw men bundled into "Black Marias" who were merely unsteady on their feet. (In one case a man was standing in a tram zone and quite obviously waiting for a tram home).

Letters, DUTCH MIGRANT. As a naturalised Aussie, may I add my voice to your correspondents, Harold Simpson and B J Pinkerton.

Having been brought up in the belief that British justice was beyond reproach, I was astonished to be convicted of a traffic offence which I did not commit and to which I pleaded not guilty. And also to hear a police constable give evidence under oath of what he saw, and which could not possibly have seen, as it never occurred. Two bystanders I asked at the time of the alleged offence told me they had seen nothing. (The only conclusion I could draw from this was that they considered it bad practice to give evidence against the Police Force.)

After I had been fined, I told the police constable in question, in a friendly manner, that I really did not commit the offence. Although he had just told his story under oath, he gave me the following reply: "How am I to remember this case after nine months?" (The hearing was deferred for nine months.)

Since this fateful day I am afraid that my rating of the sincerity of our Police Force has dropped below zero.

Letters, T Kinkead, ex-Inspector of Police. The unsupported and probably politically inspired letters appearing in your paper recently inferring that the Police Force is composed of a gang of sadists who delight in brutally bashing fellow-Australians and wickedly conspiring to send them to gaol or have them mulcted in fines on trumped-up evidence, **is a grievous slander** against a body of self-sacrificing men who have done much to help humanity and help the erring to become better citizens. The greatest evil, however, arises from this tendency to undermine by false issues public confidence in the administration of the law.

I spent 36 years in the Police Force of this State, all of it in the inner metropolitan district, and worked my way through the ranks to commissioned officer, and have had charge of some of the bigger police divisions, and I say emphatically that the police organisation is such that unnecessary violence, intimidation or corrupt practices are not tolerated by the officers or by the men under their control.

I know most of the present executive officers and I have complete confidence in their integrity. They are all men of long experience and forever watchful that the good reputation of the Police Force is maintained. I worked as a constable with Colin Delaney, the Commissioner, and I subsequently worked under him, and I am convinced that no man in the service could expect any favours from him if proved guilty of wrong-doing.

It is quite wrong to say that stipendiary magistrates exhibit any partiality towards police evidence. The police give their evidence, and whether the person charged is convicted or not is of no import to the policeman. On the other hand, the charged person has a vested interest. Is it not more logical that he would divert from the truth than the policeman would to send a fellow-citizen to gaol on perjured evidence?

It is not true that members of the Police Force are on friendly terms with magistrates, apart from the usual salutation and a salute on meeting the magistrate occasionally on arriving at the court. No other unofficial conversation takes place.

I have had cases dismissed by magistrates who were not satisfied that the evidence given by me was sufficient to prove guilt beyond all doubt. It did not necessarily follow that the magistrate disbelieved me. This often happens and people glean the impression that the police evidence was false.

Letters, Elton Lewis. In this State, the alcoholic content of liquor is twice that in England. This is why our police are faced with a much greater problem than in England, where it is possible even to drink to excess without the violent effect often noted in Sydney.

I served in the NSW Police for 28 years, and in three visits to England was able to observe personally the vast difference in the drinking habits of the two countries, as well as the greater effect our higher alcoholic content in liquor has on the individual.

Comment. A mixed bag.

BIRTH CONTROL

Dr Leslie Rumble was the spokesman for the Catholic Church in many matters. He hosted a very popular radio show in Melbourne in which he put dogmatically the Catholic Church's policies on all aspects of life. He was inflexible in his attitudes, and reflected the strict line that the hierarchy dictated.

One issue that **was coming into focus now** was birth control. Many Catholics were at this time being torn by the Church's rule that the prime reason for sexual intercourse was **for the purpose of propagation**. This meant that it advocated, in fact demanded, that the only way of stopping pregnancies was the so-called rhythm method by which women, and men, abstained from sex during her fertile period. So for almost a week each month, sex was off the menu.

Let me say, almost as an aside, that the large number of Catholic children in the world testified to the fact that this method had holes in it. Perhaps it was due to errors in forecasting, or it might have been that the temptations of the flesh could not be overcome. In any case, little Micks were running round in families of six and eight, while the contraceptive-using Protestants could only muster four or five.

This was at a time when a few people were asking what was the purpose of religion, and this questioning was showing up in reduced attendances in churches, and in the diminished position of clerics in society. That was not to say that vast hordes were rejecting religion, but it was certain that temporal forces of all sorts were gaining ground over religious.

This questioning led to exchanges such as the one reported below.

> **Letters, R W Cooper.** Let us assume the existence of two married couples, A and his wife B, Y and his wife Z. A and B are Anglicans. They are a devout couple who desire to live Christian lives and to assume family responsibilities. By the use of contraceptives they space out their family so that they have three or four children in 10 years.
>
> Y and Z are Roman Catholics. They have similar ideals and ideas to their friends A and B. By the use of their knowledge that certain times in the month are unfavourable to contraception, they space out their family so that they, also, have three or four children in 10 years.
>
> If I understand Dr Rumble rightly, and he has been correctly reported, A and B are offending against moral law and committing a grave sin. The behavior of Y and Z, however, is perfectly lawful.
>
> To me, and I suspect, may millions of devout Christians, it seems the good doctor makes a distinction where there is no difference.

Dr Rumble wanted to say something. The words he used included this pearl.

> **Letters, L Rumble, MSC, Sacred Heart Monastery, Kensigton.** May I add that Catholic principles do not say without qualification that restriction to unfavourable times is "perfectly lawful." Married people would sin by their purely selfish motives, unless there were serious reasons, medical, eugenic or economic, to justify mutual consent to abstention during naturally fertile periods in any systematic way. Without such reasons,

they would not be dispensed from accepting such children as would normally result from their marriage.

As usual, his words were full of such wisdom as to make them **impossible to understand**. But I am sure that he is affirming the position that the only right way for Catholics to avoid a serious, mortal, sin was to breed like rabbits.

Other writers added to the subject, but they simply showed **how determined both sides were**. One side said that you should enjoy sex and accept it as one of God's gifts. The other side said that if you do that, you are sinning, unless your mind is fully set on procreation at the time. I know that few of you have been in this situation, but I have heard it said that it **might be hard to keep your focus on procreation during such encounters**.

Comment. I point out that any questioning that was happening now was small compared to **a decade later when the Pill came onto the scene**. I might mention that about then, the Catholic Church held a big committee meeting of the world's Bishops, called Vatican II, and they **almost** overturned the ruling on contraception. It battled over this for the next 20 years, but in the end it did not quite make it.

When the Pill came, contraception was back in the spotlight, and the Pill's utility and its certainty made it an enormous hit.

The question then for good Catholic women was should they risk offending the Church for their own temporal pleasure, or should they still gamble month by month. Or should they cut their allegiance to the Church. I think it safe to say that there were large numbers who opted for every one of these alternatives. Also, I think it true to say that many Catholic women were not permanently fixed in their decision. They changed over time, as we all do in all matters.

Comment. Oh No! What have I Done? I have just violated the unwritten law that **no one in Australia in 1958 can talk sex, or religion or politics.**

I have just talked about **not one of these, but two of them.** Mind you, in writing the above, I was sitting firmly on the fence. Or maybe, dicing with death. Turning several blind eyes? Putting a foot in both camps?

Anyway, you get the message. I was trying to talk about sex and religion and the sensitive issue of birth control and mortal sin. So, I tip-toed through the tulips and hopefully got the message across that **the deliberations of 1958 were just the start of important society-changing attitudes.**

It brings me to an obvious change in society over the last 60 sixty years. **Everyone today talks freely about all three subjects any time they want to. In some cases**, for example, gay sex or gay politics or the failures of the churches, **the abundance of discussion can become wearing.** But can you remember how taboo it would have been to talk publically in 1958 about, say, gay sex? You might have been locked up in some jurisdictions.

ALBERT NAMATJIRA

Albert had acquired some considerable wealth, and as part of his tribal custom, many relatives came to live with him. He had settled at a place called Morris Soak, a dry creek bed not too far from Alice. He had been granted special rights by the Government in **that he was allowed to buy** and drink alcohol, and this was a privilege denied to other Aborigines.

A woman at Morris Soak was killed during a drinking session there. Albert had left a bottle of rum on the seat of his car, and was accused of the crime of supplying alcohol to other Aborigines. He was found guilty by the magistrate who also said **he was responsible for the death of the woman**. He was sentenced to six months in **gaol**.

A public outcry followed, and the Minister for Territories intervened, and Namatjira was moved to a nearby Aboriginal reserve. He was released after two months.

Comment. My bare-boned report just touches on the matter. In particular, it was evident that Namatjira suffered a great deal during the trial, and incarceration, and from the Magistrate's decision.

Shortly after his release, he suffered a heart attack. He died in August 1959.

OCTOBER NEWS ITEMS

Australian **long-distance runner, Herb Elliot**, is the holder of the world record for running the mile. He has been **offered 110,000 Pounds to turn professional, and has just refused it**. This was well received in amateur sport after the recent conversion of many tennis stars to professional status....

The relief for amateur sport did not last for long, and **over the next twenty years almost all types of sports allowed professionals**. In fact, most top level senior sportsmen in the nation are now pros.

An investigation has concluded that **police took bribes** to give towing business to certain **tow-truck operators**. As a result, **15 officers will be investigated** further. Importantly, in future a new official system of **rotation of tow-truck drivers** will be introduced.

Sydney will host its annual **week-long Waratah Festival**. Part of this **is the selection of a Festival Princess**....

The selection for this was done yesterday at lunch time in Hyde Park. Nine girls were selected, and asked to try on a "gorgeous **black suede slipper** studded with gemstones." It fitted one girl perfectly, and she was crowned Princess for the week....

She will attend **Ladies' Day** at Warwick Farm races tomorrow, and the **Royal Ballet** tomorrow night with the Lord Mayor and his wife. She was given **a fox cape stole, an evening gown and jewellery and clothing** to suit the many functions she will attend. On Saturday, she will ride the leading float in a two mile *"Pageant of Storybook Folk"* parade through the city.

The Pope of the Catholic Church, **Pius XII, died** after suffering two strokes in the last few days. After three days of balloting, **John XXIII was elected Pope**. He was a 78-year-old from Venice, and was later famous for **attempting reforms of the Church through a special Council called Vatican II**

The **"Sack" was a form of dress** that some women were adopting as **fashion**. It was extremely simple, and rested on the shoulders and amply fell down with nothing else to talk about. It could be tied in the middle, but that **gave it too much shape for some tastes. Norman Hartnell**, the designer of clothing for the Queen, said in Sydney that the sack-line was **"a monster nearly strangled at birth by masculine hatred"**. He added that the "modern version is **now slack rather than sack**, and is designed to give some definition of line."

The heat is back on over police bribery. An enquiry **in Victoria** found that **60 per cent of the special police chasing SP bookies had been corrupted by bribery**.... If that is true for **special** police, what would be the figure for the ordinary suburban or country cop?....

Would NSW police be better that Victoria's? The cat was among the pigeons, and this was true right across the nation. But the question was that emerging was not whether the current laws should be enforced, but **whether they should be changed to allow off-course betting. So here is the birth of the TAB's.**

YOUTH IN THE SPOLIGHT

It was noticeable right across Australia that its citizens after the War were more active and zest-filled than they were before the War. It seemed that this post-war generation had thrown off the conservatism and pessimism that affected the nation earlier, and were starting to say that the sky was the limit. You could see it in their attitude to churches, to sports on Sunday, to drinking laws, to their (unsatisfied) demands for new housing, **their rejection of arbitrary authority**, and their acceptance to spending generated by the nascent Hire Purchase industry. Wherever you looked, there was the question "why not?" and the follow-up "we can do it."

This turned out to be a good thing, but it had its moments of doubt. **The young lads and lasses** who had been the wartime generation **were asking the same questions and getting the same follow-up answers**. This likewise was a good thing for the vast majority, but for a minority it resulted in a lack of discipline and an increase in delinquency that was worrying for parents and for society.

Remember **the parents of these youngsters had been brought up in a far stricter regime**, and while they appreciated the greater freedom that they and their children had, they were often bemused by the devious paths that the new teens found.

We can have a glance at some situations and possible solutions. I start with the statement made by a Member of the MLC who stated in a well-publicised speech that bad conduct had its roots in the poor discipline in schools, and advocated the cane and the strap for offenders. This was a view widely held by many adults in our society. It was always accompanied by a story of how at some stage the narrator had received a bit of a licking by a teacher, and had responded by realising their former folly. This, they said, was good enough proof that corporal punishment works.

Then there were many stories that remembered the town **police sergeant** giving offenders a kick up the tail, and that again had sanctified the incipient villain. And there were stories about dads belting boys with their belts, or cricket bats, and girls sent to bed without tea by their mums. In all cases, the results were that near sainthood followed, so there was strong support for this generation of parents.

Letters, J Greenwood. The assertion that corporal punishment should be reintroduced in schools to check the growth of the "bodgie element" augurs ill for the advancement of education and penology in NSW.

I have been under the impression that enlightened thought favours elimination of the **causes** of anti-social behavior whether in children or adults and the **rehabilitation** of the delinquents rather than the infliction of pain largely to gratify the emotions of the punisher. I had hoped that man's inhumanity to man despite cat o' nine tails, keel-hauling, mutilation and other refined or unrefined acts of sadism was slowly, perhaps, but perceptibly declining.

I had even hoped that corporal punishment in schools would one day be abandoned as rather elementary for a modern trained teacher. Perhaps Mr Lawrence is under the impression that it has been.

But there were some who disagreed. **Firstly,** in the **schools.**

Letters, Realistic. Perhaps J Greenwood believes that anti-social behaviour can have its causes removed speedily and painlessly. Acts of sadism, nowadays, are more likely to come from young teenagers who have been known to use fists, boots and teeth on other young people.

In addition, some **bait** teachers, and sometimes parents, with a continual series of minor misdemeanours, the cumulative effect of which is to injure the health of those genuinely interested in their welfare. Sometimes quick action has to be taken, as J Greenwood could find out if he had prolonged dealings with some of this type under prevailing school conditions.

But **secondly**, and now moving from indiscipline to schools to more general delinquency, there were arguments that supported laying in the boot.

Letters, R E A Bennett. Opposing the advocacy of corporal punishment in schools by Mr W R Lawrence to check bodgieism, J M Greenwood talks of eliminating the "causes" of anti-social behavior and the "rehabilitation" of criminals. The only causes of anti-social behavior are the **inborn viciousness of the individual who indulges in it**, and lenient punishments which encourage him to practice that viciousness.

The policy of leniency to, and "rehabilitation" of, teenage criminals which J Greenwood advocates has enjoyed a great vogue in Britain and the USA in recent years. The result has been **a big increase in teenage crime in both countries**. The British Home Office describes the increase in Britain as "frightening," and says that a feature of it is the increase in vicious attacks, assaults and beatings.

The terrible prevalence of teenage gangsterism in the USA follows years of increasing leniency, notably the release of great numbers of criminals.

A similar trend is obvious in Australia. The alarming number of murders by teenagers here in recent years is undoubtedly due to (a) lack of corporal punishment and other strong discipline of children with vicious tendencies and (b) the knowledge that murder by a teenager will bring only a few years' gaol (or detention in some more comfortable institution) instead of execution, or life or long-term imprisonment. Murders by teenagers were extremely rare when these heavier punishments were applied.

J Greenwood's statement that infliction of pain as a punishment is "largely to gratify the emotions of the punisher" is a piece of pseudo-psychological nonsense, and an insult to healthy-minded people who want something more done to prevent crime. It could just as easily be argued that advocates of leniency to criminals do so only to gratify **their** emotions.

Finally one woman was prepared to throw the clock back, and rely on pre-war measures.

Letters, Elizabeth Kemp. As the mother of five who will one day be teenagers, and I hope not delinquent ones, I read with interest the articles which appear daily in the press on juvenile delinquency, whether to punish the young criminals or otherwise.

Isn't it possible that the answer to this problem was discovered by a Senior Judge of Brooklyn's (USA) highest criminal Court when he said, "Put father back as head of the family"?

Let him rule with judicious use of the stick for major offences plus plenty of love and firmness and forget about the possible inhibitions. Our fathers' and grandfathers didn't appear to have many. This way you'll have respect for authority.

Surely this is what the "unfortunate teenager in trouble" lacks.

Comment. I know that there would be many people who would tell me that corporal punishment does not work. Many of these people have their own suggestions, and indeed a huge industry has grown up that sometimes claims to know what should be done. Yet, and I am guessing here, it seems that, across society, delinquency and poor discipline in schools still remains as big a problem as it was in 1958. Perhaps even more so.

What do you think?

ANOTHER SIDE TO SP BETTING

I mentioned earlier that SP betting was conducted illegally in every pub in the nation every time a horse, dog, or trotting meeting was held, and for all fight nights. Most of the churches opposed this gambling, and they influenced the majority of politicians who were not anxious to lose their votes.

But the huge sum of money that was wagered, and the number of bettors, testify to the fact that the populace in general wanted some form of legal betting. To support this, a writer offered this interesting opinion.

Letters, John McGirr. As a person with considerable knowledge of country towns and as a member of the Liberal Party and a delegate to the State Council, I wish to dissociate myself from statements made at the annual convention regarding starting-price book-making, in which I feel at least 90 per cent of the adult community participate at some time or other.

Unfortunately, owing to the policy of the Cahill Government regarding freight, apart from the rural industry which cannot be shifted, **the only other industry left in most country towns today is the**

SP betting industry. I would say that in any State country electorate at least 500 are employed directly or indirectly in operating this industry, and when one takes into consideration their families, it is readily seen that a large voting strength is involved.

Finally, I do not favour legalised SP, but feel **the ideal system is the tolerance exhibited towards SP**, the same tolerance which is given to bathing between sunrise and sunset and the laws in clubs and hotels.

But, once again, cries were raised against legalizing gambling. Below, a determined Rev Gordon Powell has his say. It is clear where his vote lies.

Letters, Gordon Powell, Presbyterian Church. It would be a tragedy if SP betting were made legal. Those of us who lived in South Australia during the betting shop era never want to see a return of that evil.

Before betting shops, there were 12 fine cricket teams in Port Augusta. After the betting shops came it was hard to muster two teams for a match. Premier Playford got rid of the shops during the war. Today South Australia has less gambling than any other state and is highly prosperous.

Two years ago in Christchurch, NZ, I took a photograph of the board outside one of their legalised betting establishments. The photograph shows the hours of business for six days a week. This establishment was close to a main shopping area and was a constant temptation to women with the housekeeping money.

Every time gambling is legalised it is increased. One American State after another found to its cost that legalised gambling merely produces "big shots" who not only corrupt the police, but Governments as well.

It is a policy of despair, surely, to say if some people won't keep the law, let us abolish the law. There is no future for any nation on that basis.

Letters, Golly Bain. Rev Powell's rambling collection of so-called facts makes you wonder just how logical he is.

But his last paragraph tells us that **if 90 per cent** of the people want SP betting, then the Government should do, not what **they** want, but should do what **he** wants. What a great way for democracy to function.

Comment. Whether you agree or not, his point is well made.

A CHANGE IN DIET

If you want a change from two chops and mashed potatoes for this evening's meal, I have just the menu for you. Below is a collection of good-for-you food that is **guaranteed to put hair on your chest**.

It works too, I am told, for men.

Letters, (Dr) Herbert Hyde. For more than 25 years I have indulged from time to time in eating snakes and other jungle delicacies such as crocodile's tail, locusts and portions of Africa's large mammals.

Regarding the taste of snake the matter has so far been over-simplified; as with all kinds of meat the question of quality must be considered, whether the snake was young and tender or old, tough and tasteless. Equally important is the way it has been cooked. From the descriptions given by our anthropologist at Fitzmaurice River, it would appear that even the greatest delicacy would turn into a hopeless mess in his bush-kitchen!

Furthermore, taste is individual and one cannot be dogmatic about it, apart from the fact that very few people would be unbiased, if they knew they were eating snake.

As far as I am concerned, I should say that the taste of snake is half-way inbetween fish and meat. One might compare it with a completely "degreased" eel, for both snake and crocodile meat are very lean, white and of an appetizing appearance. The taste resembles crayfish (Cape lobster) or shrimps, but is not as good.

I do not believe that there is much difference in taste between the various species of snakes as long as they have been prepared the same way. I have generally stuck to python, but on one occasion in the Gold Coast, West Africa, I ate a portion of a black cobra to prove that the meat is not affected by the venom. Many natives eat horned and puff adders.

I ate snake meat as steaks, fried in butter, which would have preserved a maximum of the original taste. Curried, both snake and crocodile meat are quite palatable; but this spicy ingredient would suppress the original taste which many, though not the writer, might regard as an advantage.

TRY, TRY AGAIN

I sired my first daughter in 1958. It is her photo on the front cover. Not a bad effort for a first go. I think I might have another crack.

NOVEMBER NEWS ITEMS

In a coal mine tragedy, about 90 miners in Canada's Nova Scotia were trapped down a pit. 19 of them were rescued after a week, but 50 are dead, and the remainder missing. The **Governor of Georgia has offered miners a week's holiday** at an island resort off Georgia so that they can recuperate....

They will all go to the same resort. Except for one miner, and his family of 12. **He is a negro, and must go to a resort separate from the others.** He intends to accept the offer, because the other 18 said **they would not go unless he does.**

Friday, November 7th. The **Tasmanian Supreme Court** made a decision in the **Hursey case**. It noted that the Hurseys had been prevented from working by picket lines on 25 separate occasions. On 11 different occasions, fellow watersiders had walked off ships and closed down operations when they attempted to work....

The Court found in that **the imposition of a levy** for the benefit of the Labor Party **was invalid**, and ordered the Waterside Workers Federation (WWF) to pay **the sum of 2,500 Pounds to each of the Hurseys**....

Menzies enthused that " it was a **day of mourning for the Communists**, and a day of rejoicing for all Trade Union members opposed to Communists." So that was the end of that. **Or was it?**

The *SMH* carried a front-page story that **200,000 people went to Sydney's beaches on Sunday**. Even allowing for the normal exaggeration in crowd counts, that is a lot of people. It reminds us of **the beach cult** that pervaded at the time. Remember when the **girls with deep suntans were considered real peaches**? No *slip, slap, slop* to spoil the fun in those carefree days.

Monday November 11th. No, it wasn't over. When the Hurseys reported for work on Monday, they could not break through the picket lines for two hours, and when they eventually joined their gang of **25 men, this gang walked off the job.** More trouble on the waterfront....

The National WWF ordered **members to work with the Hurseys** until after **a High Court appeal against the recent judgement. They did so**, but at a furious pace that left the pair exhausted. We will now wait for the High Court decision on the appeal.

TV in Australia has a new "first." It was used to stage a **"Great Debate"** between two Liberal and two Labor hopefuls in the upcoming Federal elections....

The advent of TV marked the beginning of the end of **the old style stumping round the nation by all politicians**, and their enthralling **face-to-face encounters** with booing and hooting and cheering voters in halls and parks. TV-politics was very comfortable, but **many oldies still miss the hurly-burly** of a night of bustling and abuse, always with the chance of an old-fashioned punch-up.

November 17th. **Tyrone Power**, a current Hollywood heart-throb, **died today from a heart attack.**

FEDERAL ELECTIONS

The nation was due to conduct elections for the House of Representatives and half the Senate in late November. So it was time for politicians round the nation to start kissing the proverbial babies and making promises that no one believed.

The Labor Party adopted this line. Its leader, Doc Evatt, and his followers, offered the voters a dozen monetary rewards in return for their votes. For example, more generous child endowment payments, or bigger pensions. Also, the normal commitments to cutting government waste and increasing efficiency were promised, as was a foreign policy that was really the same as that of the Liberals. The policies were so old-hat, so hum-drum, that they created little enthusiasm, and only the fixed Labor voters gave them any support.

The Liberals matched Labor every inch of the way in the generation of boredom. The difference was that Menzies, with nothing to say, actually said nothing. Granted he did stump round the nation holding meetings and pouring scorn on his vocal opponents, but his policy was to stand on his record.

He reasoned that in the last eight years he had brought peace and prosperity to the nation, and that this contrasted with most other parts of the world. So he went to the elections without new policies, but just the expectation that he could keep the peace and prosperity going. So, there would be no new hand-outs and no changes in direction. Just more of the same, under the same management.

One noticable feature of the tepid campaign was the emergence of the Democratic Labor Party. It had been formed by Catholics within the Labor Party, and was committed to reducing the influence of the Communists within that Party. It had little electoral success, but its emergence **effectively split the Labor Party**, and reduced its votes. The overall result of the elections could have been different had the split been papered over.

A second feature was **the continued lack of success of the Communists**. They did field a large team of candidates but attracted very few votes from outside the Party. This once again showed that while the workforce often trusted them to advocate for the workers on the job, they had no time for them when it came to running the nation. This was at a time when the influence of the Reds was starting to fall within the Unions, and this result did nothing for their cause.

In any case, **the Liberals won with a slight gain**, and the Government was retained by a self-satisfied comfortable Party.

AFTER THE ELECTIONS

When the smoke cleared, there was plenty of weeping and gnashing of teeth. The Labor Party divided into finger-pointing factions, blaming each other, though it was hard to see the difference from their pre-election behaviour. One thing they were clear on was that they were nobbled by the DLP, and so the divide with them grew deeper.

Then religion raised its pretty head. In the lead-up to the elections, Melbourne's Catholic Archbishop Mannix **abandoned the traditional role of the clergy in elections** and spoke out on the supposedly good policies of the DLP. The fact that he had these opinions caused no surprise, because he had been a force behind the creation of that

Party. What was surprising was that he expressed them in public. It simply was not done by clergy to interfere so openly in matters of State.

Because of his high position, he might have got away with this but, under pressure, he made the **big mistake** of explaining that **the views expressed were his only, and did not represent the views of the Catholic Church**. This was a bit rich, given that **for years he had been accepted as an accepted spokesman for the Church**, and obviously relished that position.

So he came under fire from all quarters. These two letters are small examples of the more moderate criticisms.

> **Letters, E Kelly.** If a leading politician told people which religion they should belong to, Church authorities would be righteously indignant. Yet Roman Catholic bishops see nothing incongruous in supporting Archbishop Mannix, who directed Roman Catholics to support a certain political party. What is sauce for the goose must surely be sauce for the gander.

> **Letters, A A Nicholson, University of Sydney.** As Archbishop Mannix has taken it upon himself to enter into political debate, he can only expect to be attacked with the weapons of the politician. A careful reading of his Grace's statement will show that it was, in fact, political. He was not, as Archbishop Young states, "talking to his people about matters of conscience."

> Unfortunately, his Grace must have known when he made his statement that it was of such a nature and published at such a time as to be a real influence to a proportion, however, small, of hitherto uncommitted Catholic voters, either through their mistaken belief that his Grace was giving a "guide to consciences," or simply through a man of his Grace's exalted and

noble position and respected stature in the community lending his name to an attack on the ALP.

No one can deny his Grace's right to do so. Any Australian citizen has the right to express his opinion and to endeavor to influence the opinions of others. That is not to say that his Grace will not be less respected by many Catholics for having done so.

I am myself of that faith, and as a supporter of the Liberal Party I hope an unbiased observer in the disputes of the Labor parties.

There was this round-about apologist for Mannix.

Letters, E Ellis. It is absurd not to expect comment in the political sphere from statements by the churches, because the nature of Communism is such that it is hybrid of revolutionary politics and atheistic materialism. **It is not the churchmen who are to blame**, but society that permits Communism to masquerade as just another political party in an honest-to-goodness democracy.

However, the real tragedy has been that men of goodwill have been divided as to how they should combat this politico-atheistic plague. Many red and purple herrings are being dragged across the comrades' tracks in the sectarian brawl, while infinitely greater issues in the triumph of Communism in China and the engulfment of the Asian democracies by totalitarian regimes are going unnoticed.

Comment. Nothing daunted, the good Cardinal carried on in the authoritarian manner as before.

CHRISTMAS CHEER IS ALMOST HERE

Christmas is just round the corner. All the normal warning signals are there to see. Soporific carols in the shops, Santas in the big city stores, salesgirls who have no idea of what's in stock and where it is. Soon the cities will be clogged with millions of little darlings on their school holidays, some of their mothers will be having such a good time that they will faint in the crush, and Dads everywhere are sharpening the axe for the rare Christmas poultry. What a lot of fun Christmas is.

But there are some people who do not enjoy the season as much as I obviously do.

Letters, Malcolm Perry. The usual atheistic celebration of Christmas is now in full swing, and the place of Jesus Christ has been taken by His substitute Father Christmas. Australia's greatest impostor and humbug who is almost universally adored by children and even adults.

I often wonder whether Mr Heffron, the Minister for Education who believes that he himself is the best Minister we have ever had, ever thinks of giving instructions to his teachers thoroughly to debunk Father Christmas in the schools, and put Christ in his place instead

If Mr Heffron is game to do this, his name will go down to posterity, and Christian people irrespective of their politics will proclaim him as a truly great man. Otherwise, he will be an "also-ran."

Letters, Ismay Bruce. I have often shared the feelings of your correspondent Malcolm Perry as Christmas comes around, especially perhaps in Australia, where the heat exaggerates the gulf between the real meaning of the feast and the commercialised figure of Father Christmas.

I believe there is no reason why we should continue to suffer like this year after year, and with a little resolution the problem should not be insoluble. My suggestion is that we continue to celebrate Christmas as a religious festival on December 25 and put "the jolly old elf" back where he belongs as **a midwinter giver of surprises and delights.**

After a little thought, I believe that few people would disagree – the Church would approve; the business world would find that people had bigger appetites for turkey and plum pudding, and more zest for buying presents in the colder days. We might even bring ourselves to write letters to our friends instead of desperately sending cards.

Perhaps June 25 would do. The exact day is not important. St Nicholas' Day is, in fact, December 5. Australia would then reap the warm gratitude of harassed housewives, parents who drag children though hot, crowded shops, perspiring Santas, in fact, eventually, the entire southern hemisphere.

ELECTRIC JUGS

Most readers will remember various devices that were once used for boiling water for tea. My own memories are of a big black kettle sitting on a coal stove. We were in the coalfields so this stove was lit 24 hours a day. When Mum wanted a cuppa, she just moved the kettle from the back of the stove on to the hot spot, and the water was boiling in a few seconds.

I know that city dwellers did not have that level of technological sophistication and instead messed around with electric jugs. As one reader points out, these clever devices had a fault in that you could not see if the water had actually reached the boil.

Letters, Anne Howard Toes. Around 40 years ago, one of the amenities provided in a holiday cottage I occupied was an electric jug. By swerving the lid, one saw at once if the water were boiling: for the rest, one simply switched off the power and poured.

In a modern jug, recently acquired, one guesses if the water is boiling, or can make certain by letting it boil to the point of splashing everywhere. Further, to heat the pot and make a solitary cup of tea entailed a Heath-Robinson routine of turning off power, removing plug from jug (two hands required), pouring, groping for and reinserting plug (two hands again), turning on power, and when the water can be assumed to be boiling, turning off power, removing plug (two hands for the third time), and pouring – all this, we are told, being in the interest of safety.

Could anything more fantastic be imagined? In an era producing nuclear weapons, radar, television, etc., the only way found to make a commonly used domestic article reasonably fool-proof is to make it more time and power wasting, less exact, and infinitely clumsier to handle.

Have we no bright young engineers or technicians who could contrive a device which, by some simple pressure as one grasped the handle, would automatically eject the plug and release the lid? Again, if a whistling lid or gauge is impracticable (and I allow that a glass lid would become obscured by rising steam) why not have a transparent jug? One should then be able to see when the contents boiled.

But once again, we have technology to the rescue.

Letters, C S Jeffrey. Some 50 years ago "Punch" showed an old lady stepping off an electric tram and asking the conductor: "Would it be dangerous if I were to put my foot on the rail?" The conductor replies, "No mum, not unless you was to put the other one on the overhead wire." The concern of those electrical engineers who make rules for the safety of the public is largely to keep electricity users from touching a live wire and ground at the same time.

We have all seen the country cottage electric jug which someone has made so much more convenient, but which is accident-free only because there are no water pipes near it. Electric kettles are more convenient than jugs, but they cost more to buy and to **repair**.

Nature gave gas its smell and the spider a dirty look, but a live electric wire is a very innocent-looking thing.

OUR CONVICT PAST

Letters, P A Linnegar. As an English visitor to Sydney may I make a suggestion? This unique city should erect a statue to **the early pioneers and convicts**. Did they not toil and sweat to lay the foundations of New South Wales? No longer should they be regarded as the proverbial family skeleton but brought from their cupboard and aired in Martin Place or some other suitable site.

Comment. I do not know of any monument to the convicts of the nation, but I agree that a few might be appropriate.

The Letter though makes me realise what a big change has occurred over the years in how we think of our convict ancestry. As the writer said, convicts were once regarded as skeletons in the family cupboard.

Sixty years later, people everywhere are searching websites and libraries to explore their family trees, and if they find a convict or two, they crow with satisfaction and tell the world. There are even societies that accept only members who have proven convicts in their lineage, and recently there was a member who was expelled for having forged his credentials just to gain entry.

Comment. Some things do change.

RESUSCITATION

Seventy years ago I did a long course in First Aid, given by Saint John's Ambulance services. It was a course, mainly for adult mine workers, on how to assist co-workers having breathing problems, though it was general enough to cover electrocution and drowning.

There, I learned to lay the person on their front, get onto their back, and with measured strokes, pump the lungs from the back. For many years, I thought that this was the very best way to proceed until mouth-to-mouth came along. I accepted this as logical enough, and anyway it was new, and supposedly widely tested, so that became a part of my tricks of survival.

But then I came across these two Letters below, one of them immensely sad. They have not changed my mind at all, but now I realise mouth-to-mouth is not so new after all.

Letters, Mary Gilmore. An American expert on resuscitation says "A resuscitation method **first mentioned in Genesis** is the most successful method of all ... This is **mouth-to-mouth breathing**."

This form of resuscitation is an age-old one used by the Aborigines of Australia and once found everywhere in the bush. In *"Georgiane's Diary"* there is an account of an Aboriginal trying to resuscitate another who had just died.

Other native peoples, continental or island, may have done the same thing, but in about 1872, father, shown how by an Aboriginal, taught us children in case one of us had an accident and became unconscious. Bush children were taught to act in a crisis in those days.

Letters, Isabel Robilliard. In response to Dame Mary Gilmore's letter, I furnish my copy of "Georgiana's Journal," edited by Hugh McCrae.

October 1851. "A hard frost, and I have been to visit our blacks, we are quambied (camped) outside the paddock fence, on the edge of Cape Schack Road. Here I found Bogie in great distress, because his son, Johnnie (aged nineteen), was dying. Every few minutes the old man would spread himself over the boy's body and try to revive him by breathing into his mouth, or else he would have him in his arms to sing down his ear, or lift up the lids of his eyes, so that he might see the day.

"At last, not being able to bear this sight, I returned to the house where, after I had rested an hour, I heard a loud wail from the lubras and knew that Johnnie had gone."

DECEMBER NEWS ITEMS

When all the votes were counted for the recent Federal elections, the Government parties now held 77 seats, two more than previously. The Labor Party held 47. **This was the largest majority since Federation.** It highlights how **the Labor Party was being split by internal matters.**

Cricket is now on-line. The English cricket started the First Test against England yesterday. The PMG Department introduced a new recorded **on-line service** to provide scores at about 10-minute intervals....

But this on-line service was delivered **by phone**. Just ring a special number and you will be told the state of play in 30-seconds.

The service was **enormously popular.** It took **49,000 calls on the first day**, at the rate of 116 per minute.

Katoomba is a small city west of Sydney and is famous as the entry to the scenic wonders of the Blue Mountains. **To encourage tourism, it has a New Year's Eve Committee** that spruces up the region for the summer months....

It plans this year to **poleaxe a 500-pound steer in the city on December 31st**. This involves **driving a spiked spear into the beast's skull and hitting a vital spot**, whereupon it will drop dead. It will **be roasted for 10 hours and sliced up and sold as cooked steaks to revelers....**

It could be that **the spear will miss the vital spot, and the beast will go beserk.** The Committee is aware of this and will take the risk. Some citizens have protested, but the Committee is determined to proceed as planned.

A tragedy is starting to unfold in Brisbane. The First Test is proceeding and Trevor Bailey, an Englishman, batted for more than seven hours for only 68 runs. **The entire team scored only 105 runs for the day.** **Such slow rates of batting will destroy the public spectacle of cricket.** Sadly, such slowness became a disease spread throughout the cricketing world, and set attendances, and interest in cricket, back for years.

In Sydney, **the Kingsgrove Slasher made his first appearances.** At his peak, next year, he would creep silently into the **bedroom of sleeping women and slash the blankets with a razor-sharp knife.** So far, he had been reported by 20 women over the last few months, mainly for peeping-Tom incidents, and **only two slashings....**

But he is still in training, and will come back seriously into the news next year. Meanwhile, Sydney women in the near city suburbs **are sleeping with one eye open**.

The Hurseys have decided to give up labouring on the waterfront. They had hoped that after the Federal elections the Government would move to protect them against intimidation. This has not happened. Now **the abuse and violence against their families has risen**, and they have withdrawn from the wharves.

Teeny bopper girls are going crazy over **hula hoops**. Yo-Yo's are keeping the boys occupied.

HIT SONGS, 1958

All I do is dream of you	Everly Brothers
Catch a falling star	Dean Martin
Whole world in your hand	Laurie London
Kisses sweeter than wine	Jimmy Rodgers
My Happiness	Connie Francis
Rawhide	Frankie Lane
Smoke gets in your eyes	The Platters
The purple people eater	Sheb Wooley
Volare	Domenico Modungo
You always hurt the one you love	Connie Francis

TOP MOVIES, 1958

South Pacific	Mitzi Gaynor Rossano Brazzo
Aunt Mame	Rosalyn Russell Forest Tucker
Cat on a Hot Tin Roof	Elizabeth Taylor Paul Newman
No time for Sergeants	Andy Griffith Don Nott
Gigi	Leslie Caron Louis Jordan
Vertigo	James Stewart Kim Novak

TIDYING UP: THE HERSEYS

We have followed these two men for months as they have been bullied by their fellow workers, as they and their families have been treated as social pariahs, and as they now give up their jobs to get some peace. While this happened, the Government could have interposed but chose not to.

Comment. It makes me wonder what it would have taken to get the Feds to act. How much worse would the situation have to become before some action was taken? Granted it was in the national interest to keep the wharfies on the job, and to intervene would have meant strikes. But to watch this happen, day in and day out, on the front page of every newspaper in the land, **and then do nothing,** shows traits in our leaders that are not at all worthy.

Many writers agree with me. The Editor of the *SMH* left no doubt in the mind.

Editorial. The two men, who for any months have borne alone every device of intimidation that union malevolence could marshal against them, are near breaking point. They are no longer prepared to continue their "long, hard, lonely fight for the freedom of the individual, with the people who should be fighting alongside us standing on the sidelines." They have criticised both the Federal Government and the Australian stevedoring Industry Authority for supineness, and few who have carefully studied the record of their persecution by the Waterside Workers' Federation, and by individual water-siders, could fail to discern at almost every point the shocking reluctance of officialdom to stand up to the union bosses.

But the Hurseys have a case, too although they do not state it, against the mass of the Australian people. This country is a democracy in which the public attitude is assumed to be governed, in any matter affecting the rights of the individual, by a fundamental concern for freedom and fair play. By every classical standard of right thinking and right action, the brutal treatment of the Hurseys when they have sought to work on the Hobart waterfront **should have produced such a wave of popular protest that the walls of Healy's Jericho would have fallen**. Protests there have been, but too many of our professed patriots have taken refuge in the silence of expediency or in the cold cynicism of political calculation.

Other hot-under-the-collar writers took up the cudgels.

Letters, H R Krygier. However, it is an undeniable fact that, day after day, the two Hurseys were singled out, abused, threatened, menaced, pushed, jostled, spat upon and assaulted with impunity while the Federal Government sat idly by.

Letters, D G Cornwell. The day the Hurseys are forced off the job for all time we shall finally have agreed to surrender our freedom as Australians to a vicious minority. We will have then betrayed nothing less than our children, our friends, ourselves. More, we will get what we deserve.

This particular fight against mob-rule is no longer a personal matter. It is no longer restricted to the Hurseys, or to union politics. We are personally involved. This is no less than a trial of strength between bullies and ourselves; between fanatical aggressors and our way of life.

Rarely before, in our brief history, have individual rights been so blatantly attacked, the individual coerced, while so many pillars of society stood disdainfully remote and aloof. And this has happened after nine years of Liberal government.

The Hurseys have every right to call those Federal Ministers to account whose cynical indifference in this matter, coupled with a belated rationalising, emphasises our imminent plight as individuals in this country.

Letters, (Mrs) Thelma Lowe. The popular public protest should be so strong that in this so-called democratic country its cry should have not only destroyed the walls of Healy's Jericho, but also have made the Ministers roll up the sleeves of their togas and dispense justice. Instead we are reminded of a certain Roman who washed his hands and handed to the people an innocent man. The Australian people now have the Hurseys in their hands.

The Hurseys have long since discovered that they who strive to realise the ideal of freedom by being their own judge will know the agony of standing alone. One wonders what has been done in Hobart, so much closer to the scene of the crime, for such brutality as has been displayed towards these two men is nothing short of criminal. Are there not in existence some democratic organisations which could, irrespective of political allegiance, take up this case, seek support from the general public and petition the Federal government to protect the Hurseys? **Is democracy becoming decadent**, or are we so insular and so immersed in our own purely personal affairs that we are indifferent to the fate of our fellows and blind to this challenge to our way of life?

Letters poured in, every one of them expressing contempt, or consternation, or fear, or anger, or frustration. The common theme was the fear that the protection for the little man, against union bosses, was non existent. If it happened to the Hurseys, it could happen to anyone. Democracy, and all it stands for, is in severe danger.

Comment. I will end this section with excerpts from two more Letters on this theme. They are outstanding for their ferocity and vituperation and clarity.

Letters, Poppy Ray Smith. The bravery of two men who have fought for a principle, which incidentally involves us all, will remain a blot on our characters should these men receive no further help.

My husband and I are just one of the multitude, but if there is any way we could help we would be happy to do so. What can we do?

Letters, L R H Irvine. As D G Cornwell points out, the Hurseys' fight is everybody's fight and it is time for us to wake up and do something about it. If we don't, the next thing could quite well be a political party in power legislating to compel people to support it.

The Waterside Workers' Federation has shown us plainly enough that there is **no tyranny like that of a militant trade-union** over its own members. It is almost incredible that what it has done to the Hursey family could have been allowed to happen, and yet nothing has been done to prevent it happening again.

Second comment. The above excerpt from the *SMH* also contained a great quote from a famous address given by Dr Evatt in Paris. "Democracy means so much that we take it for granted, just like the air we breathe. I know what democracy is because I have been brought up in Australia. **It is in our every fibre.**" For once, Doc Evatt and I see eye to eye.

TIDYING UP THE KATOOMBA KILLING

The thought of killing a steer in the main street in Katoomba got many people excited, and many of them had words to say about it.

Letters, T Bogue Atkinson. It seems that one is very much entitled to wonder if some adults ever mentally grow up. To endeavor to boost a supposedly joyous and festive occasion by planning to lead a terrified steer along a brilliantly lighted street, through a milling noisy holiday crowd, kill it before their eyes, roast it, and eat it, is to display a type of mentality that it had been hoped went out many years ago before a rising tide of kindness and protection to animals added to an increasing awareness of human dignity.

The days of bull and bear-baiting, dancing on hot stones etc., are over, both in Australia and throughout the civilised world, whether the Katoomba Revels Committee thinks so or not. As both a resident and a ratepayer of the Blue Mountains City Council, I protest most emphatically against the proposal and I am sure my opinion will be shared by most others.

In any case, I feel that it is not legal to slaughter for human consumption anywhere but within a registered abattoir. The remedy to this repellent proposal seems to lie both with the Blue Mountains City Council and the police.

Letters, B Schumacher. The plan of the Katoomba New Year's Eve Revels Committee to make the public slaughtering of a beast a part of their merrymaking seems a sickening flashback to medieval blood sports. Apart from the safety risk or Health Department regulations, a public display such as this must leave most normal-minded spectators with a sense of disgust and shame and dampen their festive mood.

Not everyone agreed.

Letters. Alf Harris. All the meat-eaters who are complaining about the butchering of a bull in Katoomba should think again. **Where does their meat come from?** It comes from the slaughter-yard.

The creature is driven from a over-stocked train into a paddock, and kept there for a few days, without grass and no water until its last moments. Then it is given tons of water to increase its body weight. Then it is lined up and, one by one, slaughtered. The bull in Katoomba might not be better off, but it will be no worse off.

If the matrons are offended by this, they can simply not watch, or they can stay away. I say this without malice but I think it is no problem if people know where their meat comes from.

I do not eat meat at all because of all aspects of killing fine beasts. If there were more public exhibitions of killing, more people would have enough knowledge to make a choice about eating meat or not. I think that as a result, there would be more vegetarians.

CHRISTMAS CHEER

It had to happen. It always does. There seems to be no way out of it. Christmas has come again. That means that little boys will run round banging drums and firing guns, and girls will scream as they pull the heads off dolls. Mums will spend a couple of days cooking over the hot stoves, and Dads will have to mow the lawn and cut the head off the old boiler in the back yard. Some people tell me it's great fun, and why should I not believe them.

And who am I to repeat the traditional grizzles? Instead, I will just delve into a little correspondence that caught my fancy.

Letters, Lance Gill. Is the tide of Christmas so firmly linked with the trite adjective "merry," one of the definitions of which in the Oxford dictionary is "slightly tipsy"? Recently I bought from a charitable organisation a sheet of stamps for attaching to Christmas parcels and letters, every one headed with the phrase "Merry Christmas." After using several, I came to a letter to a family that had just suffered a bereavement. To attach one of these stamps was unthinkable.

Are we forever doomed to the trite phrase on printed cards of "A Merry Christmas and a Happy New Year?"

Letters, Robert Guthrie. Lance Gill's letter deplores the use of the "trite adjective merry" in association with Christmas greetings. Undoubtedly the Oxford Dictionary renders among others the definition "slightly tipsy." However the first meaning given is "joyous."

Christ himself used the term "merry," in the parable of the Prodigal Son (Luke 15). Let us rejoice and be "merry" for the birth of the Christ Child means for us, acceptance, and there is joy not only in our heart but also in heaven with the Father.

Undoubtedly the phrase "Merry Christmas" has become a commonplace expression of the sentiments of Christmas; however, only where "Christ is left out of Christmas," is this term hackneyed and worn out. The term "Xmas" similarly conveys the open rejection of Christ – in fact his name is boldly cancelled.

Comment. Every year, I have the problem that I cannot ignore Christmas and so stoically I inject some cheer into these pages. This year, the above is about as much as I can muster.

SUMMING UP 1958

The major event of the year was the Hursey epic. It all started when they refused to pay a quid for the Labor Party, and the militaristic Union tried to pull them into line.

I have covered that story pretty well, so I do not need to dwell on it here. But I should mention two other sides to it. **Firstly**, as it went on over the months, it did not generate a great deal of popular involvement. Only in December, after Mrs Hursey gave a Press interview, did the nation become outraged. She told of the hardships that she and the family had suffered, and also how much the two men had gone through. This brought out the indignation shown in the December Letters.

Secondly, sad to say, the High Court in September 1959, decided the earlier Court decision on the compulsory payment of political levies was incorrect. So part of the earlier victory was reversed. Still, a happier ending, the WWF decided at that time to **make such levies no longer compulsory**, and so on this important matter, the Hurseys had a win.

The fun-filled event of the year, for me, was the raffle run by the Christian Brothers. Of all the property they could have chosen for their venture, **they had to choose a hotel.** Coupled with the fact that it encouraged half the population to gamble, it was a **calculated** demonstration of **the differences between Catholics and some Protestants**. For some reason, I chuckled over this, and **the fiery responses** that it evoked heightened my pleasure. **Some** people might **then** have told me that I would burn in Hell for this attitude, but perhaps they are **fewer in number now**.

The saddest event was the demoralisation (and soon after the death) of Albert Namatjira. The most hopeful was that the series of news events was making the white population aware of the rotten deal that the Aborigines were getting, and the starting of a gradual and grudging process of improvement.

Turning to the future, there is nothing but blue skies in the picture. That statement, of course, could be challenged by anyone who was down-and-out, or by the disabled, or even by some pensioners. To them, all I could say would be that they were far better off than in practically any other country in the world, and our existing blanket was protective enough to stop them from rotting and starving as was the case elsewhere.

So, permit me to talk about the blue skies. We were a young, vibrant nation, with a good standard of living, with good education and good health systems. We had little of the class systems and caste systems that were still a problem elsewhere. Wherever you looked, you could see prosperity and opportunity and promise in a nation that valued the freedoms that this blessed land had then. And which it still has, 60 years later.

If you were smart enough to have been born into this nation, thank your parents for their help in placing you here, and **not** at most other places in the world. Between you, you did a good thing, and I trust that your penchant for doing good things has stayed with you until now, and will stay intact for as long as you wish.

COMMENTS FROM READERS

Tom Lynch, Speers Point…..Some history writers make the mistake of trying to boost their authority by including graphs and charts all over the place. You on the other hand get a much better effect by saying things like "he made a pile". Or "every one worked hours longer that they should have, and felt like death warmed up at the end of the shift." I have seen other writers waste two pages of statistics painting the same picture as you did in a few words….

Barry Marr, Adelaide….you know that I am being facetious when I say that I wish the war had gone on for years longer so that you would have written more books about it…

Edna College, Auburn…. A few times I stopped and sobbed as you brought memories of the postman delivering letters, and the dread that ordinary people felt as he neared. How you captured those feelings yet kept your coverage from becoming maudlin or bogged down is a wonder to me….

Betty Kelly. Every time you seem to be getting serious you throw in a phrase or memory that lightens up the mood. In particular, in the war when you were describing the terrible carnage of Russian troops, you ended with a ten line description of how aggrieved you felt and ended it with "apart from that, things are pretty good here". For me, it turned the unbearable into the bearable, and I went from feeling morbid and angry back to a normal human being….

Alan Davey, Brisbane….I particularly liked the light-hearted way you described the scenes at the airports as the American high-flying entertainers flew in. I had always seen the crowd behaviour as disgraceful, but your light-hearted description of it made me realise it was in fact harmless and just good fun….

MORE INFORMATION ON THESE BOOKS

Over the past 13 years the author, Ron Williams, has written this series of books that present a social history of Australia in the post-war period. They cover the period for 1939 to 1968, with one book for each year. Thus there are 30 books.

To capture the material for each book, the author, Ron Williams, worked his way through *the Sydney Morning Herald* and *The Age* day-by-day, and picked out the best stories, ideas and trivia. He then wrote them up into 176 pages of a year-book.

He writes in a direct conversational style, avoiding statistics and charts, and has produced easily-read material that is entertaining, and instructive, and charming.

They are invaluable as gifts for birthdays, Christmas, and anniversaries, and for the oldies who are hard to buy for.

These books are available at all major retailers.

www.ingramcontent.com/pod-product-compliance
Lightning Source LLC
Chambersburg PA
CBHW070616300426
44113CB00010B/1555